BEESON
PASTORAL SERIES

MAKING
CHURCH
RELEVANT

DALE GALLOWAY
AND BEESON INSTITUTE COLLEAGUES

Beacon Hill Press of Kansas City
Kansas City, Missouri

Copyright 1999 by Beacon Hill Press of Kansas City

ISBN 083-411-822X

Printed in the United States of America

Cover Design: Paul Franitza

Library of Congress Cataloging-in-Publication Data

Galloway, Dale E.
    Making church relevant / Dale Galloway and Beeson Institute Colleagues.
        p.   cm. — (Beeson pastoral series)
    ISBN 0-8341-1822-X
    1. Church growth.   2. Evangelistic work.   I. Title.   II. Series.
    BV652.25.G375   1999
    253—dc21   99-32617
                                                                              CIP

10   9   8   7   6   5   4   3   2

Contents

111072

Acknowledgments

This book started as a series of presentations to the Beeson Institute for Advanced Church Leadership. My role as dean is to draw together hundreds of the most committed pastors in the land. As they convene at teaching churches around the country, we learn from the most exciting breakthrough pastors and leaders. We teach Beeson Institute participants how to communicate with relevance and power to today's generations. This book represents the cream of several days of power-packed training.

I want to publicly thank my good friends Bill Hybels, Walt Kallestad, George "Chuck" Hunter, and Tom Benjamin for participating with me in the training featured in this book. Your shared expertise, passions, burdens, and victories all made the sessions insightful and top-notch.

I also appreciate my Beeson Institute support team. Warren Bird serves as my editor and liaison with the publisher. Penny Ruot serves as my administrative assistant. Barbara Holsinger, Brenda Hays, Doug Penix, and others help make the Beeson Institute possible. My wife, Margi, is also a constant companion and support in our Beeson Institute training.

We are all under the direction of Maxie Dunnam, president of Asbury Theological Seminary. I could not have asked for a more supportive and encouraging friend.

Thanks, too, go to the publishing team at Beacon Hill Press, headed by Director Kelly Gallagher and editor Bonnie Perry. Your efforts to provide tools that help make the contemporary church relevant are appreciated.

Finally, a huge word of thanks goes to my longtime friend Neil Wiseman, who championed the idea of converting these conference presentations into print, and who did the lion's share of the editorial adaptations.

I hope one day to meet each person who reads this book. Good days are ahead as you take these concepts and make them your own in your unique setting.

Introduction

Lost people matter to God. One common thread that I've seen in every great and cutting-edge church is this: a passion to reach the lost for Christ. If you don't have passion to share the gospel with those who need it, you won't have vision that matches God's heart.

God is doing a wonderful thing across North America. He is challenging pastors and lay leaders to do church in creative, innovative, and life-transforming ways that reach many more unchurched people.

This book is about how to do church in new ways designed to reach the unchurched, showing the relevance of the gospel for today's—and tomorrow's—generation.

God is drawing to himself Albuquerque Al, Boston Brianna, Chicago Carlos, Dallas Daniel, Houston Harrie, Memphis Matt, Miami Melinda, New York Nina, Roanoke Rich, and Seattle Sonji. Many of them are not openly against Christ; they just do not know much about Him. And they will probably never hear the gospel if they think church is boring, superfluous, and beside the point. To capture their attention and win their hearts, the church must make sense, meet felt needs, and demonstrate Christ's love.

My good friends join me in addressing opportunities, outlining strategies, and suggesting practices to win the unchurched. We want to help you communicate the good news about Jesus Christ in ways that help those who don't yet believe to grasp timeless truths about God, discover hope for their hopelessness, and believe that a new start is possible.

Doing church in new ways never means diluting the gospel. On the contrary, new ideas can show how the gospel is indeed good news: it is attractive, relevant, demanding, and miraculous.

I am proud of the lineup of outstanding leaders in this book. They are among the most insightful Christian leaders in our time, and their friendships have enriched my own life. Each was a featured speaker at the Beeson Institute for Advanced Church Leadership. (For more information on the Beeson Institute, call toll-free 1-888-5BEESON, fax 606-858-2274, or E-mail: <Beeson_Institute@asburyseminary.edu>.)

George "Chuck" Hunter III, expert on understanding the unchurched, opens our thinking to pivotal ways to share the Savior with the secular mind (chap. 1) and explains how to decipher contemporary culture (chap. 6). Then he shows us how to make church significant to pre-Christian people (chap. 9).

Bill Hybels, Willow Creek Community Church founder and senior pastor in the Chicago area, shares his heart on how bold love enriches the believer and attracts the unchurched. He explains the important ways to intentionally give and receive love (chap. 3).

Walt Kallestad, the innovative senior pastor of Community Church of Joy in Phoenix, explains the advantageous methods of doing ministry like a missionary while taking the church public like a marketer (chap. 4). In another chapter, he shows the importance of discovering and following God's dream for a specific assignment at a particular time (chap. 7). He suggests that longer-term pastoral commitments are of vital significance in the impact of community ministry.

Tom Benjamin, Light of the World Christian Church senior pastor in Indianapolis, reminds us of our Lord's mandate to "bring the children to me." From his effective experience winning urban youth, Tom Benjamin explains how a church can make a life-transforming impact on young lives and at the same time improve the community. He then shows how a community comes to respect and attend a church that authentically cares for youth and children.

I enjoyed working with this outstanding group of leaders. My chapter on how to grow a healthy church (chap. 2) explains how quality ministry attracts the unchurched. Healthy churches will be sturdy, attractive, and competent in service to Christ and to the people He wants us to win. My second contribution (chap. 5) deals with purpose-driven assimilation as the heartbeat of church health and growth. I also discuss detailed strategies for increasing visitor retention.

The heart of the book is how to use creative methods to reach new generations with the never-changing gospel. Winning the lost is an adventure in partnership with the great Head of the Church, Jesus Christ. Your interest in this book indicates your concern for lost people. Let's trust God together to raise up a new generation of great churches whose hearts continually break with Christ's concern for their unchurched friends and neighbors.

▪ *1* ▪

DISCOVERING THE PERSPECTIVE OF SECULAR PEOPLE
Pivotal New Ways
to Communicate Christ

George Hunter III

I spent the summer of 1962 in ministry to the peoples of the Muscle Beach section of Los Angeles.

Muscle Beach, in that period, represented the most heterogenous smorgasbord of humanity I've ever seen before or since. For instance, there was the muscle crowd—bodybuilders, weight lifters, power lifters, physique aspirants, and others. There was also the beatnik element—long hair, beards—concentrated at beatnik coffee shops and art galleries; they were the ideological forerunners of the hippies. There were prostitutes, homosexuals, alcoholics, drug addicts, drug pushers. There were surfers, and there were people devoting their lives to acquiring the perfect suntan—and succeeding admirably. All together, there were about a dozen subcultures sharing the landscape. Though they did not have much communication between them, they shared the same turf. Though very different from each other, virtually all of them had one thing in common. When I referred to the message of Christianity, they did not know what in the world I was talking about! They were secular people, with no Christian memory, no Christian background, no Christian vocabulary. They were forerunners of the many people we now see in the secularized Western world.

I trace the history of the secularization of the West largely in terms of six megaevents: the Renaissance, the Reformation, the rise of the modern city, the rise of the nation-state, the rise of empirical science, and the Enlightenment—an ideological movement that swaggered into Western history with enormous confidence in human reason. Each of these events changed Western society forever.

As a result of the secularizing effects of those movements in the Western world, we have seen the unprecedented rise of secular people. This large and growing population has no Christian memory; they do not know what we are talking about.

Their lack of understanding and growing numbers can be illustrated in many ways, but nowhere more clearly than in George Gallup's longitudinal study of the American people begun in 1968. In that study, Gallup began asking people: Do you have any religious training in your background? Nine percent said no in 1968. Seventeen percent said no in 1978. Twenty-five

That makes the U.S. the largest mission field in the western hemisphere and the fifth largest mission field on earth.

percent said no in 1988, and 35 percent in 1993. Extend that graph to the present, and you have about 40 percent of the people in this country with no religious training in their background.

Add a second group. These are the folks who had some religious training, but it did not take. They just didn't get it. They can't recall it. They are not in living touch with it. It is no more a part of their thought processes than my high school geometry is now part of mine.

When you add those two groups together, you have at least 120 million people age 14 or older in the U.S. That makes the U.S. the largest mission field in the western hemisphere and the third or fourth largest mission field on earth.

In the ancient and medieval period of Christendom, Christianity influenced every area of Western life and thought, and virtually controlled the religious agenda. That era of a "home field advantage" is long gone. As a result, people are exposed to a whole smorgasbord of options, from astrology to Zen Buddhism and everything in between. Christianity must now compete for the attention, the minds, and the allegiance of people in this land as never before.

By definition, secular people are people who have never been substantially influenced by the Christian religion. Our problem, as Lee Strobel reminds us, is how to understand the mind of unchurched Harry and Mary.

In terms of a functioning description of secular people, let's consider five essential issues.

• **No influence.** Secular people are people who have never been substantially influenced by the Christian religion. Somehow they have navigated their whole lives without being impacted by the more than 360,000 congregations in North America.

• **No memory.** Secularists have no Christian memory, no Christian background, no Christian vocabulary. They possess no frame of reference for what Christians are talking about and what we commend.

• **Not "church broken."** Secularists are not church broken! If you have ever raised a puppy, you understand this rather earthy analogy. A puppy does not come into the world already knowing what to do and what not to do in the house. Secular people do not know what to do and what not to do in church. On the rare occasions when they visit church, they do not know when to stand up and when to sit down, they cannot relate to the music, they cannot find 2 Kings or 2 Corinthians. The whole church experience is an uncomfortable mystery to them.

• **No sense of the Christian adventure.** Secularists may have had some exposure to Christianity in a diluted form, perhaps on TV or in the movies. They question why thoughtful people would give time, effort, and money to such pointless activity. Or perhaps at an impressionable age, they attended a church for a while. Not understanding the traditions and practices, church seemed boring—from which they generalize about all churches!

• **No openness to traditional Christianity.** Because of those earlier and shallow exposures to church, secular people are inoculated against Christianity, or at least the form of Christianity to which they were exposed. This is one reason why the only churches reaching appreciable numbers of secular people are churches that employ new forms.

STRATEGIC RESPONSES TO UNCHURCHED PEOPLE

In *How to Reach Secular People,* I suggest what a church's strategic responses to secular people might look like.

53 out of every 100 adult Americans could not name even one of the four Gospels.

• **Inform ignorance.** Secular people are ignorant of basic Christianity. They do not understand the essentials or fundamentals. They do not know the ABCs of the gospel. Twenty-five years ago, George Gallup conducted a scientific survey and discovered that only 35 percent of all those surveyed could name four Gospels, 4 percent could name three, 4 percent could name two, 4 percent could name one, leaving 53 out of every 100 adult Americans who could not name even one of the four Gospels. It is undoubtedly closer to 60 percent now. I'm suggesting that 60 percent of Americans do not even have a superficial familiarity with the gospel as found in the first four books of the New Testament.

The strategic response to such a widespread lack of understanding may mean that a creative ministry of instruction is necessary to reach secular people. Willow Creek Community Church in the Chicago area has been stressing for years that to reach pre-Christian secular people, the agenda is Christianity 101. You cannot assume that secular people understand the basics.

• **Emphasize meaning.** Until recent times, most people sought life after death. Today, most secular people seek life before death! They seek meaning, purpose, and significance. The English philosopher Bertrand Russell observed that most serious thinking in years past was about death, and people asked questions about life after death. But today with life expectancy double what it was a century ago, with the advance of mortuary practices masking the reality of death, and with scientific medicine now providing inoculations and cures for diseases that used

Until recent times, most people sought life after death. Today, most secular people seek life before death!

to wipe out large segments of a population, more and more people are asking about the quality of their life this side of death. These same people sometimes sense they are merely existing, that they are just going through the motions of life. They may wonder whether there is any meaning or significance or purpose to their lives.

The strategic response is to explain the Christian faith in effective, clear, imaginative ways. That means using not only left-brained rational concepts but also right-brained imaginal explanations that employ analogies, images, metaphors, stories, poems, and songs. It also means helping people discover the meaning and purpose available to people who follow Christ.

Churches that demonstrate to secular people that following Christ provides meaning for their lives are getting a hearing.

• **Dialogue about doubt.** Secular people, we are learning, are more conscious of doubt than of guilt. Until fairly recent times, you could assume that people experienced guilt, for which they felt responsible, and they knew they needed divine forgiveness or atonement. Today, you meet secular people dominated by conscious, epidemic doubt. They harbor theological doubts and also doubts about the church. They are cynical, suspicious, and skeptical about the church's agenda, priorities, and credibility.

As a strategic response to secular people's doubt, the church that engages in meaningful dialogue will have a hearing with many unchurched people. The more dialogic and relational you and your church people become, the more effective your outreach to secular people will be. The church that learns to engage in patient, understanding, two-way conversations in response to people's questions, needs, and hang-ups will be able, in time, to gather a harvest. The church that knows only how to preach at people will have diminishing effectiveness, with almost no response among the secular population.

If my extensive experience in conversational ministry with secular people is representative, I can promise that when you get in dialogue with secular seekers, you will make three remarkable discoveries:

1. You already have answers to some of the questions people ask. Your years of going to church, studying theologians, reading the Scriptures, and listening to sermons have actually prepared you to engage in apostolic conversation around many questions that secular people really do ask!

2. You do not have adequate answers for some of their other questions. That discovery will drive you to the Scriptures, to your knees, and to the community of faith. In reflecting upon the questions, you will learn much more useful theology than you could learn from many books in "desk theology."

3. You will not be able to find answers to questions around pain, suffering, and natural evil that are completely satisfying to people who haven't experienced faith. Indeed, some of these questions hound the faithful as well.

Most secularists have never had an opportunity to talk about their doubts with a Christian who wasn't judgmental or defensive in the face of honest questions. Just getting their questions out has the effect of defanging their doubts. To your surprise and theirs, such a dialogic relationship sometimes becomes sacramental to them.

• **Offer an alternative church.** Many secular people have a negative image of Christianity. Some have doubts about Christianity's truth claims; they assume that truth is the province of science and education—not religion. Some perceive what we do from 11:00 to 12:00 on Sundays as boring, and they perceive the Christian life as a rule-bound, plain-vanilla life stripped of adventure. Some think of Christianity as irrelevant; it doesn't scratch where they itch, and does not engage the issues with which they struggle.

The strategic response is to intentionally and attractively offer an alternative style of church that presents the Christian life as the greatest available adventure through contemporary liturgy and celebrative music. Offer a church that begins where people are rather than where we would like them to be. Offer a relevant Christianity that addresses their questions, their doubts, and their fears.

• **Engage the alienation.** Most secular people are alienated. They may feel alienated from the natural world, and they know we face a looming environmental crisis. Some churches respond by taking people into the world of nature again. On retreats, they get people in touch with creation. I have interviewed converts who discovered the presence of God for the first time out on a retreat in nature. The "natural revelation" engaged them through campfires, waterfalls, sunrises, sunsets, rain, animals, and singing birds.

Many secular people are alienated from their neighbors. They may be estranged from the people on their block, in their apartment complex, or at their place of work. They lack the opportunities or skills to build meaningful relationships. For this and many other reasons, the small-group movement is here to stay in society as well as church. The church of the future will not be a church *with* small groups, but it will be a church *of* small groups where membership in a small group will be even more primary than church membership.

> *ffer a church that begins where people are rather than where we would like them to be.*

Many secular people feel alienated from the political and economic systems upon which their lives depend. They understand the bumper sticker that appeared during the last presidential election: "Don't vote for anybody; it only encourages them." One strategic response is to connect Christian social concerns with evangelism. This is why a growing number of churches invite people to join them in working for justice, peace, and reconciliation.

Many people are alienated from their work. What they do for a living is only a means to pay the bills, provide college funds for the kids, and make retirement possible someday. In response, some churches are pioneering the Protestant doctrine of vocation, that shows how everyone has a calling.

• **Protect anonymity.** Many people who visit a church want their space and even anonymity, at least at first. They have been confronted before, often by Jehovah's Witnesses or Mormons. So when they come to church, they often come defensively; their guard is up.

Sensitive churches allow the seeker to have anonymity for as long as he or she wants it. They work with people at their pace and at the pace that God is orchestrating in their lives.

• **Encourage self-worth.** Most secular people are afflicted with a low sense of their own dignity and self-worth. A few have inordinately high self-esteem, while a few have volatile self-esteem.

Two biblical doctrines offer incredibly good news to these secular people.

The first doctrine is that we are created "in the image of God" (Gen. 1:27). Most secular people do not know they are created in the image of God, just a little lower than the angels, for God's special purpose, and for a relationship with Him. Many secular people have taken Darwin so seriously that they are much more inclined to think of themselves as intelligent beasts.

The second theme that engages secular people with self-esteem problems is the doctrine of justification. It communicates the good news that God accepts us just as we are, warts and all, and we can discover this unconditional acceptance through trusting faith.

• **Proclaim the Kingdom.** Secular people often believe that history is out of control. They view it as an endless series of large-scale shocks, frightening surprises, and nervous threats, like volatile job markets, stock markets, worldwide terrorism, and germ warfare.

Our response is found in the Christian doctrine of the kingdom of God. One day the will of God will be done on earth as in heaven, and we are invited to join the movement that advances history toward that goal.

- **Offer freedom from addictions.** Many secular people experience out-of-control forces in their lives like obsessions, compulsions, and addictions. We have become an addictive society. Perhaps a majority of secular people are handicapped by some destructive addiction that has hijacked their lives. Their addiction is destroying them and those around them incrementally over time.

Many church leaders are familiar with this brute reality. We all know people with addictions to alcohol, or nicotine, or prescription drugs, or illicit drugs like cocaine. We know people with food addictions, gambling addictions, and sexual addictions. We know people addicted to moneymaking or to spending it! We know people with relationship addictions—that morbid clinging dependency upon another person.

The 12-step recovery group movement is here to stay. It is already the underground awakening of our time. More people are discovering the grace of God for the first time through 12-step recovery groups than through all the explicit evangelism programming combined. That is why two or three aggressive churches in virtually every city now offer scores of 12-step recovery groups for people with various addictions. These effective churches are growing and thriving as they transform lives.

- **Seek lost people.** Secular people are like sheep without a shepherd. They do not know how to find the way by themselves that leads to the life they want.

Samuel Shoemaker, the midcentury Evangelical Episcopalian, wrote a poem about pre-Christian people with no Christian memory as being like blind people feeling along a wall, knowing there must be a door somewhere that leads to life, but they cannot find it by themselves (see Afterword). The strategic response, Shoemaker said, is for enough of us to be willing to spend our lives standing by the door to help them find their way in.

PIVOTAL COMMUNICATION WITH SECULAR PEOPLE

From many interviews with converts out of secularity, let me share 10 principles for communicating Christianity to secular people.

• **Begin with active listening.** J. Russell Hale wrote a marvelous book titled *The Unchurched: Who They Are and Why They Stay Away.* He conducted interview research with people in the eight most highly unchurched counties in the U.S.A. One of his significant conclusions was that many secular people do not feel that the church understands them, much less empathizes with them. He also discovered that most people cannot hear until they have been heard. Effective Christian faith sharing seems to be about 80 percent listening and 20 percent talking.

• **Begin where they are.** Discuss their questions, their needs, their doubts, and their struggles. Then you correlate the relevant facet of the gospel to their question. What you hear (through active listening) now influences what you say.

• **Explain basic Christianity.** Use language they understand. Do not use theological language, ecclesiastical language, the language of revivalism, nor the language of the Holiness Movement. If you doubt it is possible to speak the gospel in common language, I commend the *Good News Bible, Today's English Version,* in which the entire biblical revelation is phrased in the language of the ordinary people of America. Use that Bible as your model.

• **Begin with the Gospels.** Some parts of the Bible are not immediately useful with many unchurched people. Some shy away from the Old Testament because they associate it with legalism, or the letters of Paul because they associate them with dogmatism. But many secular people are attracted to Jesus and what He said.

Thus, you may need to begin with one of the Gospels. Which Gospel? If you are in conversation with a Jewish person or a Muslim, begin with the Gospel of Matthew because part of Matthew's rhetorical burden is to demonstrate that Jesus is the promised Messiah.

If you are in ministry with people who are particularly highly educated, or philosophically inclined, you might begin with the Gospel of John. Saddleback Valley Community Church in Orange County, California—the county with the highest average educational attainment in the U.S.—introduces all of their people to the Gospel of John and hold many Bible studies for seekers, focusing on the fourth Gospel.

If you are in ministry with hard-living people whose lives are out of control, begin with the Gospel of Mark. Mark demonstrates that Jesus came to set people free from whatever evil powers terrorize, threaten, or destroy them.

With all other people, begin with Luke. Willow Creek immerses its people in the Gospel of Luke. Campus Crusade based the *JESUS* film on the Gospel of Luke.

This is part of our reality—that we must reach out to lost people with the parts of Scripture that speak most specifically to their situation.

• **Practice the miracle of dialogue.** As I mentioned previously, you will discover you have some answers; you will discover you can find some other answers; and you will discover there are some questions for which there are no intellectually satisfying answers. The fact that seekers are getting some questions answered, that they are vocalizing their questions and doubts, and that they are experiencing acceptance from you in the process, is what will be used by the Holy Spirit to help you make a difference in their lives.

There is virtually no instant evangelism for secular people.

• **Count on cumulative effect.** As our society becomes more secular, people need more learning and relational experiences before becoming believers. For the average convert, it takes between 30 and 40 experiences over weeks, months, or years—most usually months—to work through the Christian possibility and cross over the line for good. This means there is virtually no instant evangelism for secular people. Rather, as Willow Creek and other apostolic churches have discovered, a *process* of evangelism takes place over time. Secular people become converts as a result of the cumulative effect of a number of messages, a number of conversations, and a number of experiences over time.

• **Use creative redundancy.** Effective churches say essentially the same thing over and over again in many different ways.

Paul demonstrates this principle in his Epistles. While the doctrine of justification is the core of several Epistles, he never unpacks it exactly the same way twice.

*A ssimilation precedes
commitment for more and
more secular people.*

• **Assimilate before commitment.** Over the years, I have asked new converts, "When did you feel as if you really belonged, you were wanted, you were meaningfully included?" More and more, boomers and busters are saying, "Well, I felt like that before I ever believed. I felt like that before I ever experienced faith. I felt accepted and wanted before I ever considered joining the church." Indeed, they say, "That's what helped me to believe and take the risk of faith." Assimilation precedes commitment for more and more secular people.

• **Christianity is more caught than taught.** That is why we want to bring people into fellowship and community. We know the evil one does not stack things in the secular world to help people find saving faith out there. The church is the realm of redemption, especially the small group that provides belonging and friendship in which people can explore the possibilities of faith. They are more likely to catch faith by getting involved with the message, or a fellowship, or in service than by detached observing. Increasingly, churches see part of their mission as creating the kind of climate, worship, body life, conversation ministries, and involvement opportunities that permit seeking people to discover faith.

• **Clarify facets of the gospel.** Be clear about the facet of the gospel you want them to discover first. Be clear about your goals for people as disciples of Christ. Sam Shoemaker, decades ago, often invited people to conduct "an experiment of faith." This experiment meant living for a specified period of time doing the things Christians do, living as though Christianity is true; people could thereby discover for themselves whether Christianity is "self-authenticating." In a modification of this concept, Willow Creek invites people to connect "the wisdom of

Scripture" to one area of their life, like their marriage, for a season; people learn they can trust Scripture, so maybe they can trust God.

THE RISKS AND ADVENTURES OF WINNING SECULARISTS

Reaching secular people will deplete your strength and stretch your soul. But it will also pump your adrenaline and drive you to seek direction from the Holy Spirit. It will light an amazing contagion in your life and church that only comes from introducing people to Christ at the front lines of contemporary culture. The adventure is like winning a football game on the enemy's turf. Prevenient grace goes before us every time. And our sense of fulfillment is immense.

Lee Strobel from Willow Creek Community Church suggests the incredible excitement of apostolic ministry: "No adventure is greater, no enterprise is more exciting, and no effort is more worthwhile than communicating Christ to an irreligious person."

•2•

TEN CHARACTERISTICS OF A HEALTHY CHURCH, PLUS ONE

Developing Quality Churches That Attract the Unchurched

Dale Galloway

Any church, regardless of its size or location, can help fulfill Christ's Great Commandment ("Love the Lord your God with all . . ." [Matt. 22:37]) and Great Commission ("Go and make disciples of all . . ." [28:19]).

Those who do so become healthy churches, just like what happened in Acts 2. People loved each other, and they reached out. Their healthy congregation attracted the unchurched.

> They devoted themselves to the apostles' teaching and to the fellowship, to the breaking of bread and to prayer. Everyone was filled with awe, and many wonders and miraculous signs were done by the apostles. All the believers were together and had everything in common. Selling their possessions and goods, they gave to anyone as he had need. Every day they continued to meet together in the temple courts. They broke bread in their homes and ate together with glad and sincere hearts, praising God and enjoying the favor of all the people. And the Lord added to their number daily those who were being saved (*vv. 42-47*).

A healthy church can be defined as one growing both in numbers and in quality, both in winning people to Christ and in growing disciples into strong Christians. If a church is not growing in these ways, then something unhealthy is present that needs to be corrected.

In my life I've transitioned a traditional church into a growing church, and I've planted two growing churches. Through my "20-20 Vision" seminars and the Beeson Center where I serve as dean, it's been my privilege to visit dynamic, cutting-edge churches across the continent. Here are the most common characteristics I find in these healthy role models:

Characteristic 1: A Clear-Cut Vision

Church health and growth begin with vision. George Barna says that only 4 percent of senior pastors have a clear-cut vision for their church. That's so unfortunate, because a church will never rise any higher than its vision.

A leader without vision is like an octopus on roller skates: it goes everywhere and nowhere. If a TV antenna can be tuned to find an invisible signal and translate it into a focused picture, then why can't Christian leaders, as God's instruments, likewise discern the leading of the Holy Spirit and then communicate a focused idea of what the church should be and do?

A great work for God always begins with vision. It is the starting point and should be the focus for everything else a church does. If a proposed ministry or activity does not fit the vision, it should never be launched.

> *ision centers on the marvelous things God has done and will do.*

Vision involves far more than a committee putting together a mission statement. A clear-cut vision gives focus. It keeps you on target, telling you who you are, what to do, and what not to do. It shapes the goals you set, both short-term and long-range. Vision centers on the marvelous things God has done and will do.

The leader's job is to influence key people and bring them together around God's vision. That may be the most important thing you do as a pastor!

I get inspired by the yarn about two mountain men sitting on a log. One was a muscular hulk of a man, and the other was short and small. The small man said to the bigger man, "There are some big bears up there in the mountains."

"Yep," said the big man.

"If I was a big man like you, I'd go up there and git me one of those big bears," the small man challenged.

"Yep." Then the big guy said, "Guess what; there are a lot of little bears up there in those mountains too."

He was right. No matter where we live and serve, we can find spiritually needy people whom we can reach for Christ. You don't have to be a big church in a major population area first. Every pastor has the passion-motivated potential to reach people wherever they are.

A compelling vision can raise any church above mediocrity. Visionary leaders see God's future work so clearly that it's as good as already done. Vision keeps leaders from being bogged down in the stuff that comes from the day-to-day tyranny of the urgent.

In the opening months of starting New Hope Community Church in a drive-in theater, we had no money, no property, and few people. The way we cast vision and built momentum was by talking about how great God is and how He would build a great church that reaches the unchurched thousands. We believed God would use us, few as we were at the time, to touch the city of Portland, Oregon, in a significant way.

"Look at this life God has changed." Nothing is more powerful in building people's faith than a constant flow of changed-life testimonies or answered prayer. By focusing on what God has done, a leader can build anticipation for what He wants to do next.

If you're not excited, no one else will be. My wife, Margi, used to meet with the choir on Sunday mornings before the worship service. She might read a verse like "serve the Lord enthusiastically" (Rom. 12:11, TLB). Then she'd have the choir raise their hands and say, "Boy, am I enthused for Jesus!" When people are enthusiastic for Christ, they build a positive attitude of faith.

Many more insights about leading with vision can be found in the Beeson Pastoral Series book *Leading with Vision*. In that helpful volume, Maxie Dunnam, John Maxwell, James Earl Massey, and Elmer Towns join me to help Christian leaders energize and achieve their vision.

Characteristic 2: Passion for the Lost

Passion fuels vision, and vision carries out mission. If your vision is biblically centered, it will lead you to be outreach focused.

Cutting-edge churches have different styles and looks, but their senior pastors all share one common characteristic: passion. When I listen to them, I get big tears in my eyes for the lost. I like to hang around passionate people because it builds my excitement. The same thing happens for the people of those churches!

Rick Warren, author of *The Purpose-Driven Church*, says, "A commitment to the Great Commission and a commitment to the Great Commandment will grow a great church." What a combination! If your vision is biblically based, it will fulfill both of those desires of God. The Great Commandment and the Great Commission incite passion for ministry.

What can you do if your passion is low? Passion can be cultivated. Choose to be passionate about what Jesus is passionate about. A church must begin with "want to" before it can move to the "how to."

Lost people matter to God.

Does it break your heart that people are lost? Are you passionate about what Jesus is passionate about? Lost people matter to God. Jesus said, "I must work the works of Him who sent Me while it is day; the night is coming when no one can work" (John 9:4, NKJV). Elsewhere the Bible reminds us, "Now is the accepted time; behold, now is the day of salvation" (2 Cor. 6:2, NKJV).

What gets your attention gets you. Your priority, whatever that is, will characterize your ministry. If you don't have passion, pray about it. When you have a passion that is burning out of your inner being, you will have an urgency about the gospel.

I was with a group of Beeson pastors in the office of Dr. Sundo Kim, pastor of the world's largest Methodist church. "I'm sorry I can't be with you today," he told us as he greeted us. "I'm so excited because we're going to have 1,000 people here today who are taking military training. I'm going to give them lectures on character, morals, and family life. And I'm going to weave in the gospel all day long."

He continued, "Last year when we did that, many families visited us, were converted, and joined our church. I'm very excited about the possibility of that happening again."

Even though Pastor Kim has 85,000 members, he is still passionate for the lost.

The next day, he told me, "On January 1 [this was March], I set a goal that we would bring 100 new people to our church every Sunday."

They had four services that Sunday. I preached those four services, which started at 7 A.M. and continued through the middle of the afternoon. At the close of each service, Pastor Kim invited all the new people to come down front. Then he personally shook their hands and welcomed them. He might have reasoned that with so many members, 100 more was not so important. But he followed the pattern of Jesus by believing every lost person is important to God.

When the day was over, he smiled and said, "We had 130 new people today. We have not missed that 100 goal any Sunday since we started on January 1."

That's passion for the lost. Passion comes from always remembering that people matter to God. If you have passion in your soul to reach the lost, you *will* find a way to reach people.

Characteristic 3: Shared Ministry

Robert Coleman's influential book, *The Master Plan of Evangelism,* shows how Jesus spent time with a few people whom He could develop into leaders. One of my applications from that book is this: Only what we share multiplies. To get the maximum impact, concentrate on the few. As John Maxwell says, "In order to be effective, we must nurture all, equip many, and develop a few."

History teaches that when laypeople are involved, churches thrive. When elitist clergy take over, a church dies.

One of the biggest deterrents to church health is the elitist attitude of some clergy. In many churches, the hoops laypeople must jump through to do ministry are either too many in number or too confusing to be identified.

In recent years I got to spend a day with Steve Sjogren and his Vineyard church staff in Cincinnati. They are good at giving ministry away. They have so closed the gap between clergy and laypeople that it was becoming hard to find a difference. As a result, the table discussion that day was who should be called "Pastor."

At New Hope, a Jewish man named Chuck Goldberg came to Christ, became a group leader, and began to mentor other group leaders. When one of "his" men died, the family wanted Chuck to conduct the funeral. Here was a lay pastor leading the funeral service, while four staff pastors from New Hope sat in the congregation.

We pastors had truly shared the privilege of ministry with Chuck. I believe the New Testament Church functioned like that.

The more people take ownership in ministry, the higher their level of satisfaction.

Similarly, every cutting-edge church today is high on giving laypeople permission to do ministry in accordance with their spiritual gifts. The more people take ownership in ministry, the higher their level of satisfaction. As the Bible teaches in a section about spiritual gifts, the work of pastors is "to equip the saints for the work of ministry" (Eph. 4:12, RSV).

Christian philosopher Elton Trueblood in *A Philosopher's Way* traces shared ministry back to Jesus: "The Christian faith is not made up of spectators listening to professionals. . . . The notion that a Christian must minister arose, in the beginning, from the example of Christ himself. Early Christians realized that they were called to minister because Christ ministered, and they were called to follow him. 'For I have given you an example,' He said, 'that you should do as I have done to you' (John 13:15, NKJV)."

Of course, Christ's followers need training. They need guidance and direction. But one of the most joyous days of my ministry was when I learned we had four ministries at New Hope that I did not know existed. It was rewarding to see that as ministry is shared, it multiplies. Cutting-edge churches learn to help people discover their gifts and place them in service opportunities according to their giftedness instead of just filling jobs.

Take the long look. Don't merely force people into a job where they don't fit. Help them discover who they are in Christ. Use and develop their gifts in ministry to the glory of God.

Characteristic 4: Empowered Leaders

John Maxwell says, "Everything rises and falls on leadership." Build leaders, and they will build ministries. Build leaders, and they will build churches. Since so much rises and falls on leadership, every successful church needs more leaders.

You don't become a leader by burning the candle at both ends, pushing yourself until you learn to do the work of 10 people. Rather you should strive to lead 10 people to do the work of 10, and 100 to do the work of 100. The ministry of your church must go beyond the personal reach of its pastoral staff.

Every successful church needs to have a leader-making system. Find any church where leadership development is happening and leaders are being grown, and you'll discover that it became that way on purpose. Leader making does not happen unless you intentionally emphasize it.

Healthy churches sooner or later develop three primary levels of leadership.

a. Personal leadership of pastor. Developing your ability to lead effectively is a lifetime process. I am still learning how to be a leader. In the Beeson Institute for Advanced Church Leadership training, hundreds of pastors and I are learning ways to develop ourselves as leaders.

Only as we lead more effectively will our churches break out to new achievements. This kind of personal leadership development must be a lifelong quest for pastors.

b. Leader of leaders. The second level a pastor should cultivate is learning to be a leader of leaders. I train and coach Tony and Marta as they lead others. As pastor, I make time to be with home group leaders, Sunday School class teachers, women's care circle leaders, worship team leaders, youth group leaders, and others in leadership roles.

c. Leader of leaders of leaders. The third level is one most pastors don't consider. When you become a leader of leaders of leaders, your church will minister on an exponential curve. Your church's impact begins to explode because of what takes place through ministry multiplication times multiplication times multiplication.

Sadly, the senior pastor may sometimes be the biggest roadblock to leadership development. If you have to be involved in everything in your congregation for ministry to take place, your church will never go any farther than you can reach. That's a sobering idea—that a pastor might put a ceiling on ministry.

You will not see any large church grow without a leader who learns to develop three levels: (i) leaders (ii) of leaders (iii) of leaders.

Lay leaders not only must be given opportunities to serve but also must be empowered and developed. I learned the importance of intentional development from a lay pastor in one of our small groups. He said, "There are two people in our group who are going to make wonderful small-group leaders, but they don't know it yet. They are new Christians. I might scare them away if I ask them to be my assistant or apprentice. So last week I said to Jim, 'Here, would you make this phone call?' I showed him how, he did a great job, and I affirmed him. I said to Maria, 'Would you lead the prayer time in our small group?' I showed her how to do that; she did it well, and I affirmed her." He was developing group members one step at a time to become group leaders.

Effective churches today are those who think multiplication.

Effective churches today are those who think multiplication. Every church today has limited resources, even those we might look up to as the biggest, fastest-growing, wealthiest, or most evangelistically fruitful. Wise leaders learn how to multiply the resources that God has already entrusted to them, such as:
—Multiplying themselves through developing others as leaders
—Multiplying the workers in the great harvest
—Multiplying small groups by raising up apprentices
—Multiplying the number of worship services to reach more people
—Multiplying the use of buildings

—Multiplying the ways resources are used

—Multiplying the church through church planting

Many years ago a friend challenged me by asking, "How do you multiply your sermon preparation?"

"What do you mean?" I responded.

"Do you write your sermons out? Do you print them for people?"

"Never did that," I answered.

"Since you are doing all that preparation, why not print them and pass them out to people? Why not multiply the effect of the work you are doing?"

So I started printing my sermons and passing them out to people. Soon nearly 7,000 printed sermons were distributed each week. People gave them to friends, and we mailed them. We multiplied the preaching resource. If I were doing the same thing today, I would have put these sermons on the Internet.

From my sermon preparation, I had accessed much material I never delivered orally. I used this to write a small-group lesson on the same passage and same subject. The idea is to multiply whatever resources you have.

Characteristic 5: Fervent Spirituality

"Never be lacking in zeal, but keep your spiritual fervor, serving the Lord" (Rom. 12:11). One evidence of spiritual fervor is an ever-deepening life in Christ. Leadership teams in healthy churches carefully pray and strategize ways to bring people to new and deeper levels of commitment.

How do you intentionally bring people to new levels of commitment? Rick Warren's church uses a baseball-diamond model. Bill Hybels talks about the five Gs (grace, [personal] growth, [small] group, [spiritual] gifts, and [financial] giving). Walt Kallestad positions Community Church of Joy in Phoenix as a mission outpost. Everything they do is a mission to reach people for Christ.

For us at New Hope, the membership class brought 60 percent of the people to a commitment to Christ. We had additional means for helping people grow in their prayer, stewardship, and other areas of spiritual maturity.

For 23 years, I tried never to think of New Hope Community Church as a church, but as a mission for reaching unchurched secularists. Everything we did was a vehicle to reach people for Christ—that's fervency of mission. I tried to live and lead by the concept that the church is not a fort to retreat into, but a mission to transform the world.

he church is not a fort to retreat into, but a mission to transform the world.

It's important for me as a leader to keep going deeper in my own spiritual walk. Every time I go to Korea (nine visits so far), I walk away feeling as if I'm still in kindergarten when it comes to prayer. There's a reason why David Yonggi Cho's church is the biggest in the world. Last time I took a group of leaders there, we watched 22,000 people praying. Churches like these have taught me much about my own need to follow Christ more closely. In cutting-edge churches, prayer becomes the lifeline.

I visited the Church of the Resurrection in Kansas City when it was only seven years old and running 2,500 people in worship. I was impressed when Senior Pastor Adam Hamilton told me they had 300 people in an intensive United Methodist training course called the "Disciple Bible Study" program.

It's also important for the people you raise up in leadership around you to be committed to ongoing maturity in Christ. As this "company of the committed" presses forward, to use an Elton Trueblood expression, they will invite the rest of the congregation to new spiritual thresholds.

Think about the next levels of commitment and how you help people move there. How do you bring people to a higher level of commitment in prayer? How do you bring people to a higher level of stewardship? How do you bring people to a higher level of living their life out in mission and ministry?

Push yourself and your church to order your life together by Rom. 12:11. Fervent spirituality matters. It is an exciting challenge that will develop a balanced, healthy church—a church that grows.

Characteristic 6: A Flexible and Functional Structure

Is it important to have structure and organization? Yes,

everyone needs a bone structure—but you don't need to go around showing off your bones!

The purpose of organization is to mobilize people to accomplish the tasks we're called to do. The third chapter of Nehemiah shows how to organize and mobilize people to accomplish a God-given task. Healthy churches streamline whatever level of organization they have in order to get the results they're after.

I have yet to find a church that can't find a way to make its structure work, even within its denominational polity. John Ed Mathison, for example, inherited all kinds of committees when he became senior pastor of Montgomery, Alabama's, Frazer Memorial United Methodist Church. According to his book, *Tried and True,* his solution was to get together a vision and planning group. This Joel Committee, named for the Old Testament prophet who encouraged the old to dream dreams and the young to see visions (see Joel 2:28), influenced all the other committees.

As you adjust and refocus the structure of your church, you might need to become more skillful about introducing change. Lyle Schaller says, "The number one issue facing Christian organizations on the North American continent today" is "the need to initiate and implement planned change." My observation is that effective leaders in healthy churches spend about a third of their time managing conflict and change. If we are going to get the spiritual results we seek, we have to understand change and learn to manage it—pain and all.

Back in the 1960s, when the civil rights marches were happening, Billy Graham was leading a crusade at a stadium in Charlotte, North Carolina. He took down the ropes that designated segregation. According to his book *Just As I Am,* he said, "Our meetings will never have that again, ever." He took that kind of stand, even though the head usher and others quit.

He also had conversations with Martin Luther King and questioned, "Should I come march with you?"

King replied, "In the stadiums, you have all this influence over the Whites; but if you come and march, you will lose some of that influence. Stay in the stadiums, and in the long run, you will have more influence over more people."

The point is this: if, as a leader, you get too far out in front of your people, you will lose them. But you must stand firm on nonnegotiable issues. Knowing when to stand firm and when to change is not always easy, but it is a necessary skill.

As pastors, not only must we understand what it is we want to change, but also we must know our people. We lead at the pace they will follow. We try not to get so far out in front that we are there all by ourselves.

All churches are changing—for the better or for the worse. No one can stop it. How many churches can get all their people

> *All churches are changing—*
> *for the better or for the worse.*

together at the same hour? Not many. And yet, hundreds of churches still operate in the frame of mind that everybody has to get together at the same time and place.

Life isn't like that anymore. Effective churches today have to change, developing ministry in new and different structures. Tomorrow's church will find the people of God doing the work of God seven days a week.

Characteristic 7: Celebrative Worship

Worship is a matter of the heart. It's a response to God, based on who He is and what He's done. Worship is a wonderful, marvelous mystery. There is nothing greater in this world than to be in a worship service where your spirit meets with God's Spirit. That is the high moment in the community life of the church.

When the Holy Spirit comes, the deepest needs of people are met. Bring people into God's presence, and their deepest longings will be met. Different styles of worship reach different groups of people.

In preparing a church to worship Almighty God, we must ask intelligent and tough questions such as:
—What's the purpose of our worship?
—How do you keep growing the people you have in worship?
—What generation are we trying to reach?
—What are the needs of the people you're trying to reach, and how can you meet those needs?

—How much participation and involvement will we invite?
—How do we engage people in worship?

Cutting-edge churches that are reaching people today are culturally relevant in their music and in their preaching. Calvin Miller's *Marketplace Preaching* and Sally Morgenthaler's *Worship Evangelism* provide good examples of this concept.

Mike Breaux is transitioning Southland Christian Church, Lexington, Kentucky, to be more culturally relevant. When some of my students interviewed him about the change process, he said: "While we have used a great deal of sensitivity, there's a certain urgency that motivates us. We ask ourselves, What's the worst thing that can happen to Christians who want the 'same old, same old' at church? They might not like the changes, leave, and land in another church. But what's the worst that can happen to those who don't know Christ because the church won't make the changes necessary to reach them? They could go to hell." That motivates us.

He knows how to put the issue in context. We must make ongoing adjustments to keep reaching and touching people through celebrative worship.

Characteristic 8: Connections in Small Groups

Once, when I conducted a seminar in Springfield, Illinois, a participant made this fascinating comment: "In the 1960s we would intentionally bring someone into the drug culture by taking them to a small group. We'd meet at a home, sit in a relaxed atmosphere, make newcomers feel comfortable, pass a joint, and they'd get hooked. Ever since I became a Christian, I've wondered, Why doesn't the church use small groups to accomplish its mission—to evangelize and reach people!"

Many churches are doing just that. According to Ralph Neighbour, 19 of the 20 largest churches have strong small-group ministries with a primary purpose of evangelism. If groups are relational in focus, they'll reach both churched and unchurched people.

Cutting-edge churches are ones that know why they have small groups. You need to think through the "why" of your small groups. At New Hope the purposes of our Tender Loving Care groups have been:

1. Evangelism
2. Discipleship
3. Pastoral Care
4. Community
5. Leadership Development

The most effective evangelism today is through friendships. A lot of people could be reached if we'll raise the awareness of the relationships we already have in our life. We could reach a lot of these people by inviting them to a small group with potential friends in someone's home.

Big things happen in small groups. Christian community is not merely one person caring for 10 or so. Rather everyone is

> *ig things happen in small groups.*

both a caregiver and someone being cared for. Healthy small groups don't feature just one person teaching, but everyone serving as both teacher and learner. In a group, everyone is both a minister and someone being ministered to.

One of the biggest jobs of a pastor today is getting people connected. If they don't assimilate, they'll leave through the back door, no matter how good the preaching, music, or children's ministries.

Many people are isolated, lonely, and live long distances from extended family. Once an individual participates in a small group, he or she connects to the Lord and the church. The small group becomes like an extended family. The time and need for small groups is now.

Characteristic 9: Seeker-Friendly Evangelism

Healthy churches, without exception, are very intentional about evangelism. There are dozens if not hundreds of faces to evangelism. Cutting-edge churches do evangelism in many different ways. They are willing to experiment with new paradigms to find out what works today. Here are a handful of examples:

—Need-meeting ministries. Meet people at their point of need or pain, and you'll have no shortage of people. At New Hope Community Church we had some kind of group for every human need or pain you could name. When you reach out to people in a meaningful way, they will respond.

—Events and seminars that attract the unchurched. These become natural points of entry for the church.

—Small groups as a natural bridge for doing friendship evangelism.

—Servant evangelism. Everyone welcomes acts of kindness. As Steve Sjogren, author of *Conspiracy of Kindness* and *Servant Warfare,* says, "Small things done with great love will change the world."

Seeker-friendly evangelism is culturally aware. It does not force people, but it enters into their lives in meaningful and loving ways.

To increase the intentionality of evangelism, I suggest a church might consider using the strategies often used to plant new churches, such as the idea of building up to the launch Sunday. You could use that approach to reach a high level of contacting many new prospects for your church. I have seen some churches do that very effectively.

Some churches are building intentional outreach into their small groups. Once a month or so they will say, "Next week we are going to bring new friends to our group." They plan the lesson that way. They prepare for the new friends. It often works.

In one of my classes last year, we began listing ways to do evangelism on the board. In no time, we had written 20 different strategies. There may be at least 20 more. So the question is not *how* to do evangelism, but *do* you do it?

Characteristic 10: Loving Relationships

Jesus said, "By this all men will know that you are my disciples, if you love one another" (John 13:35). The greatest need any of us have is for love. Effective churches have been meeting that need for 2,000 years.

I once knew a pastor who was not well educated or especially gifted. But he genuinely loved people. So wherever he pastored, he always had people who were growing in Christ, and his churches always got bigger. He just loved people.

Leaders will be more healthy if they build their ministries and lives on loving relationships. People around us will be more healthy, spiritually and emotionally. Our ministries will prosper. If our love for God and for people is lacking, everything will be out of sync.

> *If our love for God and for people is lacking, everything will be out of sync.*

Do you love people? Do they know it? Do you practice loving people, even difficult ones? Some pastors love their church but hate people. A loveless pastor and a loveless congregation are never pleasing to the Lord or attractive to the unchurched.

I am by nature a task leader. About 20 years ago, I took as one of my life verses 1 Cor. 14:1: "Make love your aim" (RSV). I learned through great personal upheaval and tragedy that I must grow in love with those closest to me: my spouse, my children, my staff, my leaders. That modeling will then be copied throughout the church. As the love chapter (1 Cor. 13) teaches, ministry is nothing unless it's done in love. People will commute any distance to find a loving church that has substance behind its statements of "We care" and "We're glad you're here."

Donna, a widow at New Hope, had raised her son by herself. She belonged to one of our ladies' small groups. Back in 1987, one of the members said, "Donna, you look yellow. Have you been to a doctor?" She answered that she couldn't afford insurance.

What does a loving family do in an instance like this? They took up an offering, gave her the money, and said, "Go to the doctor."

The medical examination found a serious problem with Donna's liver. Without a liver transplant in the next six weeks, she would die.

Doctors told her that specialists at Baylor University, Waco, Texas, could do the operation for $140,000. The situation looked impossible.

Soon the women in the small group made an appointment with me to ask if the church could do something for Donna. I was troubled. We were just finishing up a building campaign, and we were still $400,000 short. I was convinced everyone was financially tapped out. I was feeling tremendous pressure, wrestling with it nightly, often sleeping poorly. I feared I would go down as the pastor who oversaddled the church with discouraging debt.

As I prayed, the Holy Spirit said to my inner conscience: "Help her."

I had told myself, "Don't get involved," but as I prayed, the Holy Spirit said to my inner conscience: "Help her." I told God I would. Immediately a creative idea came into my mind to call this "Save My Mom." Then another idea came to mind: to involve a lay leader, Tom Peterson, whose business was widely known across our city. He agreed to be honorary chairman. Another friend agreed to give six weeks of his life to organize people.

On Sunday, I laid the need before our people. In response, they gave $60,000 in cash. I didn't believe they had that kind of money!

The next day I received an invitation to testify with Donna before the Oregon legislature. They were dealing with the issue of people who couldn't afford insurance. The largest newspaper in the state took a photo, put it on the front page, and labeled it "Save My Mom."

People started bringing jars of money from bars. Little kids brought allowances. Local TV stations joined the publicity. We raised $220,000 in seven days.

Donna, check in hand, went to Baylor. There she was cared for by a small group that God had already prepared for her. We put the excess money in a trust fund that generates funds for her medications. Now, more than a decade later, you'll find Donna on Sundays singing in the New Hope choir.

For years, when people looked at our large facility on the hill, they'd say, "You're the church who cares about the widow." They don't comment on the lovely new facility, they didn't care how we sweated over building payments, and they'll never know how our people sacrificed and stretched. Instead, the Holy Spirit took our relationship with Donna and used it to multiply our ministry to lots of people who were needy for Christ. What a joy to love people in Jesus' name.

No one could even buy that kind of publicity. Something greater than any of us was at work. "Greater is he that is in you, than he that is in the world," says 1 John 4:4 (KJV). That same Holy Spirit can take your church to new pinnacles of health.

Plus One—Evaluate Your Church Continually

To these 10 important characteristics another must be added that affects all the others: Evaluation. This health factor is strongly significant in any kind of work, but especially for the church.

Evaluation teaches us how to watch for blind spots. It is easy to do things over and over without thinking about their impact. It is possible to use spaces frequently and not see scuffed walls, dirty carpets, or messy clutter. It's possible to believe your church is friendly because you personally feel welcomed and loved there.

I no longer believe the old adage "If it ain't broke, don't fix it." If that were the case, then cars would never become safer. Technology would not introduce time-saving shortcuts. Efficiency improvements would not be suggested. Overlooked needs would remain overlooked.

All organizations, especially churches, will deteriorate if left on their own. A helpful evaluation exercise is to list areas that need improvement. Be specific. Then work on that list as if it were a "to do" list. The quality of your church will increase, and impressive improvements will quickly take place in amazing ways. Learn from the past, and apply what is learned to the present to make the future better.

Cutting-edge churches gather feedback for evaluation from visitors and members—their customers—and act decisively on what they discover from the feedback. Some churches mail a self-addressed evaluation with every visitor's letter; the responses are amazing and helpful. Those churches ask questions like:

—What did you notice first?

—What are your lasting impressions?

—Based on your experience as a first-time visitor, would you return?

—If yes, why? If no, why not?

Another way to do evaluation is to visit other cutting-edge churches to find out what works for them. What you learn will probably not be useful as a cookie-cutter approach to your church, but such a visit opens your eyes to new possibilities, new ways of thinking, and improving. Sometimes evaluation encourages you because it helps you see how well you are doing in many areas of ministry.

Evaluation in the pastor's membership class was always useful to me at Community of Hope Church in Portland. To find out what impacted people, we asked questions like: Why did you come here for the first time? Why did you come back to church? What about our church needs to be improved? I liked to teach that class myself so I could keep close to the new people and hear their evaluations and suggestions.

Every phase of ministry needs evaluation—preaching, fund-raising, visitor follow-up, music, condition of facilities, welcome at the front door, and more. Be tough on evaluating yourself; then others will be more willing to take part in the process.

I always feel stretched to new levels of effectiveness when I read Roger W. Babson, business leader of another era, who said: "There isn't a plant or a business on earth that could not stand a few improvements—and be better for them. Someone is going to think of them. Why not beat the other fellow to it?" (*The Forbes Book of Business Quotations*, 445).

Evaluation and implementation of needed improvements will make your church great and effective and fun to serve.

Checklist for Improvement

Score your church from 1 to 10 (10 being the best) on each of these health characteristics. No church ever rates a perfect 10 in all of them. Where are you strongest? Where do you need to work most?

	Self-score
1. Clear-cut vision	1 2 3 4 5 6 7 8 9 10
2. Passion for the lost	1 2 3 4 5 6 7 8 9 10
3. Shared ministry	1 2 3 4 5 6 7 8 9 10
4. Empowered leaders	1 2 3 4 5 6 7 8 9 10
5. Fervent spirituality	1 2 3 4 5 6 7 8 9 10

 6. Flexible and functional structure   1 2 3 4 5 6 7 8 9 10
 7. Celebrative worship   1 2 3 4 5 6 7 8 9 10
 8. Connections in small groups   1 2 3 4 5 6 7 8 9 10
 9. Seeker-friendly evangelism   1 2 3 4 5 6 7 8 9 10
10. Loving relationships   1 2 3 4 5 6 7 8 9 10

■3■

BOLD LOVE

Magnetic Attraction for Seekers and Believers

Bill Hybels

Some wonder what goes on behind the scenes at Willow Creek Community Church. Because love stands at the center of our message, we want our staff relationships to experience and model Christian love. Willow Creek is a church, a biblically functioning community, where bold love is given and received. We believe bold love impacts ministry and sets a healthy emotional climate for satisfaction in service.

For example, staff members still slide notes under each other's door. Let me share smatterings of notes I have received from fellow team members. One ends this way: "I cannot imagine doing ministry without your understanding and friendship. This event has been another peak experience for me, which I will treasure for a long time. I absolutely love doing this redemptive adventure with you."

Another note read: "Bill, thank you. What you are doing this week is such a beautiful thing to behold. God is doing it again. He is filling you up with His energy, words, vision, and strength. Your loving friend in Christ."

Such notes are not out of the ordinary. There is a steady flow of loving interaction and support between us here at Willow Creek.

I write about as many notes as I receive. Certainly I cannot speak authoritatively about all concentric circles around Willow Creek Community Church, but loving attitudes and deeds are becoming standard fare where I operate. This work of God at Willow Creek goes forward with love, acceptance, and grace. That's as it should be, and that's what we want.

CATCHING UP AND ENJOYING IT

I regret that it took me half of my ministry life to wake up to the supremacy of love. I memorized 1 Cor. 13 as a kid. Many Christian leaders know these passages extremely well: "Love is patient, love is kind, and is not jealous; love does not brag and is not arrogant, does not act unbecomingly; it does not seek its own, is not provoked. . . . [Love] bears all things, believes all things, hopes all things, endures all things. Love never fails. . . . And the greatest of these is love" (vv. 4-5, 7-8, 13, NASB). I cannot explain why it took so long for me to understand the message of that incredible passage of Scripture. But I am now catching up and enjoying it.

Jesus taught us that love will be the main measuring rod by which our lives will be assessed. On days when I think clearly, I realize I do not want to be remembered as a person of vision, or one who achieved great goals, or one who led a big church. I would much rather be remembered by my wife, children, friends, and the flock of God as being a person with an extraordinary capacity to love. Great pastors love people.

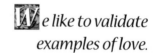

We like to validate examples of love.

Here's an example that underscores my point. It is the kind of thing we try to notice at Willow Creek. We like to validate examples of love. John Ortberg, one of our teaching pastors, started to describe the last four steps in a seven-step strategy, but one of the props was out of order. As he spoke, I thought, "Props are goofed up. John's hung. Oh, no." I knew John was going to be surprised when he turned around. Then I thought, "Oh, if he makes a biting comment about how someone messed up, there's going to be embarrassment and hurt feelings." But when John noticed the visuals were out of order, he laughed and said, "You are just trying to test me, aren't you?" He gave a soft, affectionate answer without blame.

When I saw him later, I said, "John, your reply was classy and loving. Instead of making a stinging comment, you turned it around and had fun with it. You protected the crew who are working hard to help you. And listeners saw through a window into your soul that you are a loving man." Such a response can only come from a loving leader who is committed to developing loving people.

Once we had a conference when one of our vocalists was up singing. In the middle of the song a disturbed attender whose medication was a little unbalanced left the congregation, climbed on the platform, and stood next to her. It was an uncomfortable moment for everyone.

Though the vocalist did not understand what was happening, she simply changed hands with her microphone, put her arm around this troubled young woman, finished the song, and walked off with her new friend by her side. This simple act communicated the power of love and acceptance.

SETTING THE RELATIONAL TEMPERATURE

Nothing compares with love among believers. An expanded capacity to love is the best gift you can give your church and family. It can revolutionize your ministry, attract new people, and enrich your own life.

Let me say it again—I was in church work a long time before I awakened to the fact that love has to be fundamentally what I am about and what the church is about. I need to continually increase my capacity to give and receive love. As pastor, I need to set the relational temperature of the amount of love that flows in the circles of my influence. I have to increase my capacity to give and receive love and express it inside and outside the church. And I must take responsibility for setting a loving temperature in the church.

ESTABLISHING INTENTIONAL REGIMEN

All of this means that since Jesus gave us the Great Commandment to love God with all our heart, soul, mind, and strength, and to love our neighbor as ourselves, then we must increase our capacity to give and receive love. We need an intentional program for increasing love just as we need a workout regimen to be muscularly or cardiovascularly healthy. We need a plan to develop greater hearts of love toward our people.

If I asked you, "What is your plan for increasing your capacity to give and receive love," how would you answer? If love is the greatest, if love is what God wants more than anything else, and if the world needs more love—what is your workout plan to make it happen? What is your strategic plan to increase love in your life and church? Let me share some issues I am working on for my own life.

DRINK OFTEN FROM THE FOUNTAIN OF GOD'S LOVE

If my capacity for giving and receiving love is to increase, I have to regularly drink from the fountain of the love of God. Remember the passage that says, "We love because he first loved us" (1 John 4:19)? That teaches that I am never going to increase my love capacity until I increase my capacity to receive love from God. I think about this a lot. How can I drink more effectively from the fountain of the love of God?

This is painstakingly practical. To get me closer to God's love, I listen to worship music CDs. There are mornings when I know I am overcommitted at the start of the day. Sometimes I know it is going to be a rush from 5:30 A.M. until 10 that night. When I think maybe I have bitten off too much, I remind myself that I am likely to be dangerous by about 10 or 11 A.M. My RPMs will be too high. I will be short with people. I will speak too fast. I am going to say, "Give me the bottom line." I know where that takes me because I have been there before. I realize I will bruise people if I do it that way.

*To get my day started right,
I must drink from the
fountain of the love of God.*

So to get my day started right, I must drink from the fountain of the love of God. I have a small sound system in my office and a bunch of CDs. I put my feet up on the credenza, lean back in my chair, put in a worship CD, and I drink from the fountain of the love of God.

Another source for me are the writings of Henri Nouwen. I have bought nearly everything he has written. I read his books over and over. He helps me drink from the fountain of God's love.

Certain psalms are other places to find God's love. Psalm 45 gets me in touch with Him.

Some folks have not expanded their capacity for love in years. They have not increased their ability to give or receive love. To those dear people I want to say that there is not going to be an increase unless you drink more from the fountain of the love of God. You have to find a way to put yourself near that fountain so that you have a heart of love every day.

After you have experienced and demonstrated such love, you help encourage it in your leadership team, both with professional staff and lay leaders. In leadership settings, you can get candid about a spirit of love. Then when you are in leadership meetings where someone starts pointing the finger and saying, "I think that is a lousy idea," you can say, "Whoa, let's slow down and show more love. Let's back up. Let's go back to the basics here. Then we can call each other into account about love."

The starting point for deepening your spirit of love is to keep close to the fountain of God's love.

FELLOWSHIP WITH A LOVING GROUP

Another way to expand your capacity for giving and receiving love is to fellowship with a small group who will show you

Identify the most loving people you know, and get with them more.

love and expand your ability to be more loving. Hang around the most loving people you can find. Did you ever notice that after you have had a meal with extraordinarily loving people, you walk away with a hunger in your spirit that says, "I'd like to be a little more loving like them"?

Identify the most loving people you know, and get with them more. I have those people identified in my life. Then when I am with them, I ask them questions like, How did your heart get into expressing love? Who loved you so much? Was it a parent? Was it an aunt or an uncle? I know it is God, but what other factors helped you develop such an extraordinary capacity for loving and receiving love? How did you get it? How do you keep it?

Fascinating conversations often develop. One of my friends told me about her extraordinary, loving dad. In addition to the Heavenly Father, her earthly dad filled this woman's heart with love throughout her growing-up years. Once she explained, "I walk around knowing that I had two fathers who were crazy about me. So I felt loved all the time. That gives me the capacity to love others." Identify extraordinary, loving people in your life, and spend enough time with them that some of their loving perspectives and affirming ways rub off on you.

PRAY TO BE MORE LOVING

Try making your desire for an expanded capacity for love a focus of your prayer. The idea is to ask God to give you more love and to make you more loving. If we could check everybody's prayer journal, we would likely find many requests for more comfort to come their way, for problems to be solved, or for God to get them out of a problem. But I urge you to purposely pray for more love.

Try praying on a regular basis for the fruit of the Spirit to increase in your life, especially love. I pray every day for an increased capacity to give and receive love. I have learned that if I spend time each day with that prayer focus, if affects me so I am more loving throughout the entire day. The fruit of the Spirit listed in Gal. 5:22-23 helps me keep my prayers focused: "Love, joy, peace, patience, kindness, goodness, faithfulness, gentleness and self-control." What a list.

My love capacity also increases when I sing the prayer, "More love to Thee, O Christ, / More love to Thee!" (Elizabeth Prentiss).

INTENTIONALLY CONFRONT "OUCH" SITUATIONS

Confrontation may seem a little risky, and it is. But in circles where the relationships are close and sometimes stressed—like a church staff—try this on a one-on-one individual basis for an extended period, maybe a whole afternoon. View it as an opportunity to get to know the individual better—his or her concerns, cares, and victories. Include questions in your discussion like, "What are the circumstances when I am most likely to hurt you or when you are the most likely to hurt me?"

In other words, what do we do that is most likely to make each other say, "Ouch"? I sometimes say to a staff member, "What are the attitudes and behaviors I exhibit that make you think 'Ouch, that hurt me'?" Such an awareness almost always increases love, opens communication, and strengthens relationships.

In such a setting, a member of our management team once said to me, "Your capacity to love goes up or down on the basis of how your weekend message is coming. So if I need to see you, I call your administrative assistant to find out how your message is coming. If she says pretty good, I come up. If she says it is slow, I stay away."

What an indictment that was for me.

Loving confrontation works the other way too. One management team member sometimes gives me an ouch with his sarcastic sense of humor. Though it is supposed to be good humor, I often feel the barb. That individual has no awareness of this problem, but he needs to know so he can increase his capacity to give and receive love.

Talking about these ouch factors helps everyone improve, and as a result, bold love increases in your staff and church. But it is not likely to happen without a specific and safe plan being developed where it is safe to speak about ouch factors. And the leader must take the lead to foster such a climate of openness, trust, and acceptance.

Learn to Express Love

You probably know how difficult this challenge can be from personal experience. Many of us feel love for others but do not feel comfortable or know how to express these feelings. One of my goals is to help people get their love out of their hearts into someone else's heart. To do that, I always start with myself.

Some of us think when we feel love for a family member or a ministry team member, "I ought to express this love," or "I ought to do some loving deed." But for some mysterious reason, an automatic editing process takes place inside us, so our good intention gets choked off, and our voice is mute.

Why Does It Seem Risky?

"I am not going to do that," you might reason. "I might express it wrongly. I might cause a misunderstanding. I might create a monster I'm going to have to feed." When we fall into this skewed pattern of thinking, let's ask ourselves an important question: Does expressed love ever hurt anybody? Of course, the answer is no.

For the longest time when I got serious about being able to give and receive love, I felt the love of Christ for other people through me, but I was unwilling to take risks to express it. I came out of the Dutch Christian Reformed subculture, where the idea was "buck up." The unexpressed communication taught us, "Let's not get touchy-feely, nurturing, and all that stuff. We've got a job to do. God is in charge of everything, so don't worry about it." Many of us grew up in homes and churches like that, so we feel emotionally tongue-tied and unresponsive.

I was so confused about expressing love that I actually convinced myself if I felt love for another person, that was about the same as expressing it. Let's get realistic. If you feel love and do not express it, the other person is still walking around not knowing how you feel. He or she gains no benefit from unexpressed love.

Follow the Pattern of Jesus

While studying the way Jesus expressed love, I finally crossed a line in my life. I said to myself, "I'm tired of not expressing love. I have to change." At that point, I concluded, "I can no longer blame my background. I cannot blame my church. I cannot blame my family. This is my life. This is my spouse. These are my children. These are my friends. This is my staff. This is my church. I have to take responsibility for what I am doing with the unexpressed love I feel for them in my heart."

So I started to say, "I love you."

I felt like an absolute fool the first few times I did it. I felt uncomfortable and strange. To say to Lee Strobel, "Lee, I really love you, and I'm glad you are on our team." Or to say to Lori Peterson, who has been one of our elders for 20 years, "Lori, I love you. You are a sister in Christ, and I think about you in loving, sisterly ways. I want the best for you, and I pray for you."

But the freedom this has brought! Now it is a regular part of my vocabulary. I am proud my kids are comfortable with that now. Every phone call, every time Todd or Shauna goes out the door, "Love you, Dad." I answer, "Love you, kiddo." "Love you, Bud." Every time.

S ooner or later, you must decide if you are going to be an expresser of bold love.

Sooner or later, you must decide if you are going to be an expresser of bold love. You must decide if you are going to deprive other people of the gift of the love of Christ you feel for them. Or are you going to take the plunge and increase the joy you give and the satisfaction you feel?

CROSS THE LINE AT A DEFINING MOMENT

So much of life is determined by decision points. We call them defining moments. I lived on the limiting side of love for a long time, but I finally stepped over to the other side.

I want to challenge you to walk across that line, too, so when you see your wife, husband, son, daughter, or team member, you say, "I love you." You will be amazed at what that does. The whole atmosphere around you will change.

Many people comment on the loving atmosphere around Willow Creek Community Church. It is not an accident. Neither is it an aroma that comes and goes. It has taken years of helping people grow in their capacity to drink from the fountain of the love of God and then challenging them to speak of that love to each other. In this process, we have even learned it is hard to get ugly at an elders' meeting when we start by spending time building community by saying "I love you" to each other.

THE POWER OF A NOTE

I also need to express love and affirmation in writing. Some of us are auditory, so when we hear "I love you," it is settled and done. But others need something in their hands so they can look at it again and again. I so much love to get notes and letters that I have a desk drawer dedicated for keeping such notes. Then when I need encouragement, I pull them out of my desk and reread them.

The power of a love note is incredible. A couple of years ago, we were doing a training conference in Hamburg, Germany. My daughter, Shauna, was studying at the time in London. Since we had not seen each other for quite a while, I flew her over to Hamburg for a dinner and a part of the conference. She stayed overnight in the hotel with me but had to leave the next day to go back to school. When I got back in my room after she left, I found this note on the pillow: "Dad, I love you so much. This is one more of the many memories we share together. Thank you. I am proud to be your daughter. There are many people at this conference that are thankful for you and owe much to you, but no one more than I. I pray for you, and I will pray for the team for the rest of this trip." It was signed, "Your Daughter."

What kind of gift is a note like that to a dad? What kind of gift is it to a daughter when you write a note back? What kind of gift is a similar note to a spouse? What kind of gift to a staff person or lay church member?

Enjoying the Journey

Of course, we all have hills to climb and a world to win. But the time has come to cross the line of silence. It's time to say we

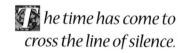

he time has come to cross the line of silence.

are no longer willing to sacrifice togetherness and community on the altar of a great cause. We need to tell ourselves if there cannot be heart and love in the efforts, we do not want to take the hills anymore. If we cannot be a loving group of people enjoying the journey and giving each other love along the way, then the work is too hard and the accomplishments are too hollow. Without love, ministry gets too mechanical and shrinks our hearts in the process.

TOUCH THOSE YOU LOVE

The power of touch comes from Scripture. Jesus was the master at giving an appropriate, loving touch. He wanted to convey love to kids, so instead of waving at them, He would stop. He would hold them in His lap and touch them.

Though Jesus had the power to do drive-by healings, He didn't. He touched people. He touched the eyes of a blind person. He touched a leper who had seldom been touched. He showed that massive amounts of love could be conveyed through an appropriate touch. A hand on the shoulder, a handshake, or a friendly hug often makes an incredible impact on another person.

I was leading a staff retreat when I asked the group to each think of an unforgettable childhood experience he or she could share. One great big guy stood up and said his most important childhood memory was riding in the front seat of the family car with his mom and dad on vacation. He said, "I remember it so vividly because my mom would be stroking my leg and my dad would pull me under his arm. Life just did not get better than that."

A brief, appropriate touch can convey a lot of love. Of course, you know the boundaries between an encouraging and a sensual touch. Some of us are paranoid about that. I am not a big hugger, especially with strangers. But let's remember that a loving, appropriate touch can communicate a lot of love.

DO SMALL ACTS OF KINDNESS

This one is fairly easy. Scripture says in Eph. 4:32, "Be kind and compassionate to one another"; and in 1 John 3:18, "Let us not love with words or tongue but with actions and in truth." I was on an around-the-world speaking tour, and it was a rough trip. When I came back, I landed past midnight.

Lynne picked me up at O'Hare. Though I always go in through the garage door, she said, "You must go in the front door of the house tonight."

I said, "Not now."

She said, "Trust me; go in the front door."

I went in the front door, and she said, "We have to go wake up Todd."

I said, "Let's let him sleep."

She replied, "No, no."

So we woke Todd. He sprang out of bed and said, "Oh, man! I've got something to show you, Dad."

He took me out to the garage. While I was gone, he had

painted the garage walls, hung some pictures, and installed part of his sound system. He knows I like to wash my car and hang out in the garage. He had redone our garage as a gift to me. When I told him I was deeply touched by his gift, Todd replied, "Dad, it just took me a couple of half days. It's a little thing."

"Todd, every time I pull in this garage, I will think of a son who did such a loving thing for me," I said.

Think about it. You know many small kindnesses that would gladden the hearts of people close to you. You know their recreations. You know the kind of things staff members love to do. You know what would be special to your kids. It only takes a few minutes to be thoughtful and take action so you can say, "During my day I was thinking about you. So here is what I did."

CARRY OTHERS' BURDENS AND ENJOY THEIR VICTORIES

This means entering into the joys and sorrows of those around us. This one comes right out of Scripture: "Rejoice with those who rejoice; mourn with those who mourn" (Rom. 12:15).

I do not know of anything that more closely bonds hearts than someone who says, "I would not think of missing this party. I will be the first one to celebrate with you. I would not think of not being a part of your great victory."

The same is true of sorrows and pain. At Willow Creek, we were about four days away from Easter and behind in our preparations. Then our drama director's mother passed away unexpectedly, and the funeral was to be held in Minneapolis. The programming team felt terrible that they could not attend the funeral.

The leader came into my office the day after the mother's death and said, "This is not good. I understand that we have to do our Good Friday and Easter services. But it is a violation of community for us not to be with Steve at his mother's funeral."

"Let me make a couple of phone calls."

I called several board members and said, "Could we allocate some money to charter a small airplane to get our folks up there to attend the funeral and come right back so that we can do the work?" It was a short conversation, because the board members said, "Absolutely!"

We chartered a twin-engine aircraft, and the team went up

there, helped Steve bury his mom, flew back, and went to work. To this day, when Steve writes me notes sometimes, he says, "I know the heart of this church was to make sure I wouldn't be alone in that situation." I do not know if it is the heart of this church or the heart of Christ. But as members of the Body of Christ, we rejoice and weep with each other. We do the mountains and the valleys together.

In the early days of the church, when my dad died over in Michigan, scores and scores of people made the 165-mile drive to stand with me. You remember those things the rest of your life.

Make Your Church a Community of Bold Love

Let me paint a beautiful picture for you. Can you imagine what would happen if every leader in your church took personal

> *Can you imagine if every leader in your church would double his or her capacity to give and receive bold love?*

responsibility to regularly drink from the fountain of the love of God? To regularly interact with loving people who could grow their heart and would pray every day, "God, increase my capacity to give and receive love"? Can you imagine if every leader in your church would double his or her capacity to give and receive bold love? Can you imagine what would happen if people whose hearts are full of Christ were saying loving things and writing loving things to each other? Can you imagine the impact if your church members offered each other appropriate, loving touches, did acts of kindness, and freely entered into each others' joys and sorrows? What kind of churches would we lead!

Bold love is not going to cost more money. You do not have to attend more conferences to begin. You do not have to negotiate or legislate. Just start. If you create loving communities like the one I have described, first-time seekers will sniff it and say, "I want in." Crusty old veteran believers whose hearts have shut down will warm up again. Arrogant people will have their pride melted.

Love changes people. Love transforms churches. Love is the greatest force in the world and the most needed component in contemporary churches.

Start the love revolution in your congregation today.

▪ 4 ▪

THINK LIKE A MISSIONARY—
ACT LIKE A MARKETER
Effective Ways to
Take the Church Public

Walt Kallestad

It was a hot summer morning when I took a Sunday break to check out another church. I had been in Iowa for a college board meeting and drove up to the Minneapolis area to visit my sister. On Sunday morning, I asked her, "Where do you recommend I go to church?"

"I think there is a church that has an outdoor worship service not far down the road, just a few blocks away," she said. "Why don't you check that out?"

"When does the service start?"

"I think it is 8:30," she replied.

So I got up early, went out jogging, got my coffee, and started out down the blocks. I was dressed pretty casually in shorts and a summer shirt, expecting to worship outside. After walking a considerable distance, I found no church, but I kept walking.

My sister certainly had miscalculated both time and distance. It was well past 8:30 when I arrived at the first structure that looked like a church. Since it was hot and humid, I was sweaty. I looked around the church grounds and did not see anything that looked like outside worship. So I walked up the front steps and looked inside. There was an usher dressed in a suit and tie with that familiar "You don't belong here" usher expression. I said, "I'm looking for a church that has an outdoor worship celebration."

He said, "No, we don't do that here." He followed with a thoughtful comment, "Obviously you are not dressed for church."

So I asked the question, "Is there a church in the area that has an outdoor worship? Maybe I got mixed up."

He said, "I do not really know. There is another church over the hill. Maybe they do that."

I started out over the hill, and it was well after 9:00 when I arrived. There was no evidence that any kind of worship was going on there, and I had a difficult time finding my way into the building. In fact, I walked around the outside of the entire building twice. Finally, I noticed a narrow corridor and thought, That can't be how you get in, but it was. So I went inside and saw a sign in an enclosed worship space that said, "Air-conditioned." That sounded especially good right then because I was wilted and hot. As I approached the door, there was a church "guard" standing there. I said to him, "I see that you are having indoor worship. I was told that there is a church in this area that worships outdoors."

He replied, "Nobody would be dumb enough to worship outside today." Well, that's probably true, I thought. It is 90 degrees with 90 percent humidity.

"It looks cool and comfortable inside there," I remarked.

"I am sorry; I cannot let you in," he answered. "The space is air-conditioned, and I cannot let any hot air in." He saw to it that I did not get in.

Two churches within a 15-minute time period let me know I was not welcome. At one it was my attire, and at the other I had intruded their space. They did not want to let any hot air in or any cold air out.

As I walked away smiling, I thought, This is rather humorous. But as I walked back to my sister's home, I became sad. My relationship with Jesus Christ was not in jeopardy because I didn't go to church that morning. But there are many people in places like that setting who try to get into a church and cannot. And though the shutting out may not always be as obvious as my experience that day, it is there, and everybody knows it. Neither of the gatekeepers I met that morning were Christ-exalting missionaries or effective marketers. Neither had the foggiest notion that Jesus intended the church to reach out to win secular people.

In fact, such an outward-focused perspective is seldom considered in efforts to attract unchurched people. Too often we assume that outsiders are welcome, but they may not feel that way. I had an experience with some of the Christian business leaders in the Phoenix area. These leaders were excited about sponsoring the *Jesus* video project for the whole city and asked if I would help provide some leadership. I challenged and shocked them when I asked, "What if it works? What if this *Jesus* video project turns the whole city to Christ, and new people start flooding the churches? Are the churches ready? What would happen if churches who are comfortable with only their own constituents got lots of strangers attending? Would the churches be ready?"

Since that time, I have been thinking a lot about the behavior of churches that are oriented to an institutional model and churches that are oriented to a mission model.

INSTITUTION OR MISSION FOCUSED—YOU DECIDE

There are some significant distinguishing marks between churches focused on institution and those focused on mission. Here's the issue: How do we learn to think like a missionary and act like a marketer?

*Evangelism in our times
often means taking the
church public.*

Evangelism in our times often means taking the church public. We as pastors and key leaders, who must thoroughly understand the gospel, seek to understand secular people and their culture so well that we, in fact, become contemporary missionaries. To do this, we must understand not only the culture in which we serve Christ but also the customs, language, and behavior of the lost. Instead of denouncing the world, we try to communicate the meaning of the Christian life to unbelievers.

We take Christ into their culture just as a missionary takes Him into foreign environments. This missionary effort may be to down-and-out people who suffer openly, or it may be to the most affluent residents in your area.

C. S. Lewis reminds us of the pivotal issues of being a missionary to contemporary culture: "If we are to convert our heathen neighbors, we must understand their culture" (*The Quotable Lewis*, 435). Developing a missionary perspective of contemporary culture takes hard work and continual evaluation, but the goal is to take Christ into the front lines where secular people live and die. As Hudson Taylor said, "There are three indispensable requirements for a mission: 1. Patience. 2. Patience. 3. Patience" (*The Doubleday Christian Quotation Collection*, 194). And I might add, three characteristics: 1. Savvy. 2. Savvy. 3. Savvy.

Since the Day of Pentecost until now, believers have been required to be missionaries to their own culture and to other cultures where the Lord sent them.

To missionary thinking must be added intentional marketing skills. Marketing for the church means understanding the basic felt needs of human beings and showing them how the gospel meets those needs. It starts with identifying unmet needs and then establishes a way to meet those needs and tells the prospective audience how the church meets those needs.

> he aim of marketing is to know
> and understand the customer
> so well the product or service
> fits him and sells itself."

Though he probably was not speaking about the church, Peter Drucker helps us with this insight: "The aim of marketing is to make selling superfluous. The aim of marketing is to know and understand the customer so well the product or service fits him and sells itself" (*Quotable Business*, 146). Perhaps the church should think of marketing as the delivery of the life of Jesus to secular people. To borrow a line of advertising from an old ad from Mercedes-Benz, "Some things are too important not to share" (Bob Briner and Ray Pritchard, *The Leadership Lessons of Jesus*, 102).

Here are several significant distinctions between an institutional church and a mission-focused church.

- **Power.** An institution-oriented church sees power as limited and controlled. A mission-oriented church sees power as unlimited and something to be shared.

An institutional congregation has a seat of power, a church board or constituent group, from whom everyone must get permission for everything that goes on. This approach controls but seldom empowers. You cannot do ministry of any kind in those settings unless you get permission. Often that power group manipulates, controls, and outrightly suspects new ideas. C. S. Lewis warns, "The descent to hell is easy, and those who begin by worshiping power soon worship evil" (*Quotable Lewis*, 483).

A church that has a mission orientation sees power as unlimited. Leaders see that their task is to give away power to enable people to effectively serve Christ. Empowerment is their goal. Empowering leadership helps congregations become healthy, robust, and growing.

- **Needs.** An institutional-oriented congregation focuses on organizational needs. Conversely, a mission model church focuses on human needs. The first question here is, What are the needs of the organization? versus What are the needs of the community and of our people? Missionaries meet needs, and marketers report how needs are met.

- **Private chaplain vs. public leader.** An institutionally oriented church sees ministry as that of a private family chaplaincy. When I arrived at Community Church of Joy, I was given an assignment to visit every member every year and to make sure that when they were admitted to a hospital, I was there to welcome them as they checked in. I was expected to follow through and care for the flock. Let's understand that effective pastoral care is essential, but much more is needed.

When a church is about mission, the pastor is seen as a public leader. I believe a church's orientation should be toward public leadership, so we not only react to the public problems but also actually influence or solve them. Let's be proactive. Let's initiate changes.

- **Meetings.** An institutional-oriented church holds many meetings. I have spent thousands of hours of my life as a pastor in meetings. When I became pastor of the Community Church of Joy, we had board meetings that lasted for four and one-half hours. In those days, we had 200 members and 87 attending the worship service. Now we have several thousand members, and our board meetings last one hour.

When I first arrived, we had four-hour congregational meetings. In recent years, we had a 10-minute congregational meeting to vote to sell our present facility, call another pastor to our staff, and give me permission to sign a $10 million loan.

What is the secret? A genuinely mission-oriented church loves ministry, not meetings. There is a whole different mind-set in a congregation when ministry has the highest priority.

*Traditions must be used
to guide us into the future
without shackling us to
the past.*

• **Future focus.** The institutional church is past focused, so the best years were yesteryears. The mission church is future focused. They are open to possibilities all around them. They work to make the future responsive to Christ. Dietrich Bonhoeffer helps us tie past and future together: "It may be that the day of Judgment will dawn tomorrow; in that case, we shall gladly stop working for a better future. But not before" (*Doubleday Christian Quotation Collection*, 206).

An institutional church overly emphasizes traditions. I have a Lutheran background, so I have great appreciation for creeds, confessions, and sacraments that represent important values. However, I have come to view tradition as a rudder and not as an anchor. Traditions must be used to guide us into the future without shackling us to the past. I see an institutional center as something like an introvert, talking to himself and judging the world by the past.

A mission center is more like a group of extroverts taking the gospel to folks around them. They talk to the world and judge themselves—quite a different orientation. The mission-centered approach attracts people and encourages many to get involved in Christian service.

• **Resources.** In an institutional church, there will be a scarcity mind-set. In those settings, the first question is often, What can I get? instead of What can I give? A mission church has an abundance mind-set that believes resources are unlimited. They believe God calls you to go. You do not wait until all the lights are green or the money sits in the bank. You start. You stand on the power of faith motivated by a dream.

Regarding human resources, institutionalism encourages rugged individualism, while a mission church encourages teamwork. The day of rugged individualism in the church and culture is past. Mission churches are committed to building great teams.

The missionary model church unleashes the power of people as it helps them work together for Kingdom achievement. Management specialist Roger Dow is right: "People connected in a meaningful way and focused on a common purpose become an unstoppable force" (*Turned On*, 206). The synergy of a team always accomplishes more than individual efforts.

An institutional church sees itself as self-sufficient. A mission-centered church views itself as needing to network and seek collaboration. An institution asks, Why? while a mission center asks, Why not? An institution stresses convenience, while a mission stresses commitments.

• **Change.** In their book *The Leadership Lessons of Jesus* Briner and Pritchard observe, "Truly innovative leaders will always be challenged by those who protect the old ways of doing things. Upon a closer look, these are usually the same people who are protected by the way things have always been done. Change always threatens some people" (54-55). Every leader has to understand why change is so difficult for some.

An institutional church focuses on the status quo, while mission thrives on change and growth. Institutional churches focus on safety and security, and they spend a lot of time dealing with those issues. A mission center focuses on possibilities and risks. Edmund Burke, the British political leader of the 18th century, offers us good advice: "You can never plan the future by the past" (*Doubleday Christian Quotation Collection,* 140). An institutional model is set up around committees, but the mission church uses task forces.

- **Imagination.** An institutional church focuses on the tried and true, whereas the mission church focuses on the imaginative and creative. In most churches, we love to talk about missionaries in third world countries—how innovative they have to be to meet basic needs, to secure equipment, and to locate supplies. Well, a missionary has to be imaginative because of his or her circumstances. But if we think about doing church as a missionary, it pushes us to similar creativity and innovation. Every congregation could immeasurably improve its effectiveness by increasing its creativity.

- **Relationships.** I see an institutional model church as focused on issues, whereas a mission model is focused on relationships. An institution is organizationally rigid, while a mission center is functionally flexible. The mission model is willing to adapt and welcomes new people and new ideas.

These paragraphs from Laurie Jones's book *Jesus, CEO* impact the need for caring, supportive relationships in our churches:

> There seems to be a divine yearning for a cooperative creative venture between God and humankind. God is looking for and is very interested in our ideas. And if God is open to our ideas, shouldn't an Omega leader be open to her or his people and their ideas?
>
> Life is about co-creation and companionship. What better way to demonstrate that than by being listening and responsive leaders?
>
> Tom Peters, author, lecturer, and consultant, reveals that 75 percent of the most recent and innovative inventions came from people outside the profession. Apple Computers, for example, was born in a kid's garage—a kid who left the big boys because they would not listen to him.
>
> Jesus was open to people and their ideas (188).

THINKING LIKE A MISSIONARY IN PHOENIX

Missionaries were special people when I was growing up. Because my father was a Lutheran minister in Midwestern rural congregations, we frequently had missionaries in our home and church. When they made their presentations, I always prayed that I would someday be a missionary. I never lost that passion—that strong commitment is still with me to this day.

God has chosen me, in fact, to be a missionary in one of the most spiritually needy, unchurched, non-Christian areas in the world—Phoenix. On any given Sunday, 20 to 25 percent of the people who attend our church are secular people. What an opportunity for a missionary, and what a challenge for a mission-focused congregation.

So when I sensed God's call to Phoenix, I thought of myself as a missionary. When I became pastor of the Community Church of Joy, it had been in existence for only two and one-half years. It was still on mission support from our denomination and still classified as a mission congregation. It was still a mission church in the minds of our members and friends. Finally in 1979, we paid $272,000 back to our denomination. Many of our congregational and denominational leaders said, "That's great; now we're no longer a mission." To which I replied, "That's not true. We will always be a mission. If we ever forget that, we're out of business; we're done."

My biblical support and mandate for being a missionary is found in 1 Corinthians, chapter 9. In that passage, the apostle Paul, one of the greatest missionaries the world has ever known, wrote: "When I am with people whose faith is weak, I live as they do to win them. I do everything I can to win everyone I possibly can. I do all this for the good news, because I want to share in its blessings" (vv. 22-23, CEV).

Those are powerful words that call us to thoughtfully and creatively engage in mission to our society. That's quite a directive. It is a different way of thinking that produces significant change in behaving. So much of what we see in this passage encourages us to connect the work of God to the culture. Thus, much of what follows is about culture, not theology. We are not changing the Bible. We are not trying to change truth. We are simply changing methods. We are not throwing out substance. But we do want to transform perspectives and viewpoints. And if we take this missionary focus seriously, it will require a new mind-set to evangelize our so-called civilized civilization.

So what are the required commitments and the challenge we will face?

1. A missionary must think "win." To think like a missionary, we must recognize that a missionary does not always have ideal circumstances. But in spite of adverse situations, missionaries seek to have right thoughts, a right mind-set, and a win attitude. A missionary must think win.

When I went to Community Church of Joy, my commitment was to reach beyond the cozy church crowd and connect with the community. I spent lots of time meeting people in the community who were not connected in any way to any church. They were secularists with no faith. The experience was exciting, humbling, and sometimes confusing.

Recently, I won a man to Christ with whom I first connected in 1978. That's more than 20 years ago. Something tragic happened in his family, so he came to church for the first time in all those years. I can tell you, it takes a lot of patience and prayer to wait for such a win, but there is also the great satisfaction in knowing God is at work through us.

Think of possible victories wrapped up in your difficulties. I sometimes think of people like John Wesley. Listen to what happened as he became serious about being in mission. In his journal he writes (paraphrased):

> Sunday morning, May 5, preached in St. Anne's, was asked not to come back. The next Sunday, May 12, preached at St. Jude's. Can't go back there either. Sunday P.M., May 12, preached at St. George's, kicked out again. Sunday A.M., May 19, preached at St. Thomas. The deacons called a special meeting and told me I could not return. Sunday evening, May 19, preached on the street, kicked off the street. May 26, preached in a meadow, chased out of the meadow as a bull was turned loose during the service. Sunday, June 2, preached on the edge of town, kicked off the road. Sunday night, June 2, afternoon service, preached in a pasture. Ten thousand people came to listen to the gospel.

That sounds like a win in the midst of trying, tough circumstances.

John Wesley traveled about 250,000 miles on horseback so he could preach. Because the established church of his day seemed geared mostly for the intellectually elite, he wanted to make a practical application of the gospel to the poor, uneducated, and unchurched. So he even used tombstones as pulpits. He tried everything he could imagine. He got his brother Charles to put gospel words to popular folk tunes. And the world has never been the same because Wesley was determined to be a missionary in his generation and setting.

Think win. Think about winning people for Jesus Christ. Certainly we realize it is the power of the Spirit that transforms people, but you must think about winning a world that is not connected to Christ or the church. Then you think about putting their needs in high priority. You think win.

When I came to Phoenix, I expressed heart passion for lost people. My consuming desire was to win those who were not connected to the church. That meant the church and I had to act differently to attract the lost secularists. To really win, their needs must sometimes even take precedence over needs of church people. In the process, I ended up going through a lot of pain and many nights of tears. Many in the church did not understand. Still I believe we have no choice; winning the lost is what ministry is. That is how we live out the incarnation of Jesus. That is making the practical application of God's truth to needy people. So the missionary thinks win.

2. A missionary must think as a visionary. The Bible tells us, "Where there is no vision, the people perish" (Prov. 29:18, KJV). Though that passage is often quoted to support many ministries and clarify many concepts, we need to consider it thoughtfully and often. What does it say and mean to us?

Someone in my church passed along this statement about vision: "If your vision is for a year, plant wheat. If your vision is for 10 years, plant trees. If your vision is for a lifetime, plant people." That's the business we are in—people. A visionary pastor understands we are in the business of helping people find wholeness in Christ.

When I talk about vision, I mean a picture of a preferred future given us by our Lord, based on an accurate understanding of God, ourselves, and our circumstances. That is what keeps a community of faith together.

Our church recently experienced the process of relocating. Across the years, we had fully developed our 15-acre campus. There was no more room. There were Sundays when we had as many as 100 cars drive away because they could not get in the parking lot. We call the land we purchased a "beachhead for mission." As we go through this transition, we have found that vision is what keeps us together. It is not a shallow scheme, but a God-inspired plan.

3. A missionary must think strategically. In the "Life" section of a recent issue of *U.S.A. Today,* there was an article titled "Mormons on Mission to Grow." That's a group who thinks strategically! They think globally and act intentionally.

One of the things that I discovered quickly as a young minister was that most churches have no idea where they are going and what is next. We could get together at a meeting and plan to get through that next month, but it was not until we developed a 1-, 3-, 5-, and 10-year strategic plan that we accomplished much. We learned that the more focused and specific our plan, the more likely it was to be realized. Peter Drucker, the management specialist, helps us when he observes, "There is nothing so useless as doing efficiently that which should not be done at all" (*Quotable Business,* 31).

If your church is to survive or even thrive in the 21st century, you must work on plans to fulfill and fund your vision. It is absolutely essential to plan well. Strategic planning is the process by which you set objectives, implement vision, assess the future, and develop action plans to accomplish your purposes.

4. A missionary must think imaginatively. Imagination is one of God's greatest gifts. Years ago Henry Ward Beecher said, "The soul without imagination is what an observatory is without a telescope" (*Doubleday Christian Quotation Collection,* 162). He is right.

Though information may be limited, imagination is unlimited. As a missionary, think through your imagination. Pour your life through your imagination so you can set the world aflame. Many people fear creativity, imagination, and innovation. But these three are wonderful friends. Get well acquainted with them.

5. A missionary must think magnificently. Lee Strobel from Willow Creek has written a book, *God's Outrageous Claims.* He writes from the perspective of a woman who had never been connected with Christ or the church. One of his main characters asked:

> Do you know, do you understand that you represent Jesus to me? Do you know, do you understand that when you treat me with gentleness, it raises the question in my mind that "maybe" Christ is gentle, too. Maybe He isn't someone who laughs when I hurt.
>
> Do you know, do you understand when you listen to my questions and don't laugh, I think, "Well, what if Jesus was interested in me, too?"
>
> Do you know, do you understand that when I hear you talk about arguments and conflicts and scars from your past, I think maybe I am just a regular person instead of a bad, no-good little girl who deserves abuse. If you care, I think maybe He cares. And then there's a flame of hope that burns inside of me and for a while I'm afraid to breathe because it might go out.
>
> Do you know, do you understand that your words are His words, your face His face. Please, be who you say you are. Please, God, don't let this be another trick. Please let this be real. Please.
>
> Do you know, do you understand that you represent Jesus to me?

When you think magnificently about Christ, you allow the power of the Holy Spirit to flow through you to others. To think magnificently means to think as your Master thinks.

Years ago Paul Rees quoted from a letter written by an Asian Christian to a missionary board: "We want many categories of missionaries, but remember, what we most want is Christ-intoxicated missionaries. Please help us to get such people" (*Don't Sleep Through the Revolution,* 126). Christ-intoxicated missionaries are needed everywhere, but especially in this fast-growing mission field here at home.

HOW TO BEHAVE AS A MARKETER

Remember to always think like a missionary but act like a marketer. Consider these suggestions:

1. Act quickly. Churches need to be more efficient. Too many committees and boards bog us down in controlling details. Streamline your policies and processes. Are you ready to respond? Are your people ready to act? Are they trained, equipped, and prepared? Keep your church on a mission alert.

xperts say that only 12 percent of the average church members in America know the mission of their church.

2. Act purposefully. A recent survey at Community Church of Joy revealed that 89 percent of the attenders know what the church's purpose is. We are pleased with these findings because experts say that only 12 percent of the average church members in America know the mission of their church. Perhaps they have not been told. Our mission is clear—that all may know Jesus Christ and become a responsible member of His Church. Our purpose, then, is to share His love with joy, inspired by the Holy Spirit, to help make our mission statement a living reality in people's lives.

3. Act with anticipation. I call this the Wayne Gretzky approach. When Gretzky, the hockey player, was asked the key to his success, he replied, "Well, most people go where the puck is. I go where the puck will be." Plan ahead. Anticipate. So when people come, you are ready to welcome, encourage, and help them grow.

4. Act like a leader. We have five nonnegotiables for persons in leadership at Community Church of Joy. When we say that all may know Jesus Christ and become a responsible member of His Church, what do we mean? We found it helpful to spell out the meaning to our leaders. If you are on our staff, on our church board, a teacher, or any kind of leader, these five things are expected:

- You regularly attend worship.
- You are involved in a discipline of daily prayer and devotions.
- You are committed to growth.

- You are committed to tithing.
- You are involved in mission.

5. Act responsibly. By responsibly, we mean a church needs to find out if what they are doing is working. If it is not, get rid of it. Too much energy, emotion, and money are used to defend sacred cows. Investigate your ministry. Evaluate your programs. Are you communicating with target groups? In Community Church of Joy, we go so far as to have unchurched people evaluate my messages. This is a part of the whole total quality management process for continuous improvement.

> *What's worse than training people and losing them is not to train them and keep them."*

6. Act like a coach. You train, train, train. I love what Zig Ziglar said: "What's worse than training people and losing them is not to train them and keep them." Do not expect people to know how to do any phase of ministry without training.

7. Act like a marketer. Church marketing is not slick hard sell but convincing conversation that invites, "Come and see." Tell everyone in every possible way that "if anyone is in Christ, he [or she] is a new creation; the old has gone, the new has come!" (2 Cor. 5:17). That is really what the gospel is about. That is what we are in business to tell. That is what people want to hear. That is what God wants us to communicate. Many people who resist Christian service assignments do not know how to do them, but it is a learnable skill. Tell it over and over. Tell it in new ways. Tell it through recently transformed people. Tell it so secularists wonder what they have missed.

MAKING MARKETING WORK IN YOUR CHURCH

The word *marketing* sounds overly commercial for many churches. Even the mere mention of the word makes us think more about Fortune 500 companies than about congregational decision-making groups or public services of a church.

But reconsider the marketing idea for your church. Marketing may be defined as an organizational focus that works to discover what unmet consumer needs can be identified, what systems can be designed to satisfy those needs, and then to communicate the solutions to persons so they know about the need-meeting product or service. Though the definition comes from the business world, it is also true for the church. When seriously applied to life, the gospel meets many unmet needs of all people including the secularists. In every age, the church is charged with the work of helping people apply the gospel to the details of their lives so they clearly understand the advantage of trading old ways for a new life in Christ Jesus. In essence, marketing is the people of God telling others where to find bread—the Bread of Life.

For the church, marketing means that members and attenders find the church so significant and helpful that they tell neighbors, friends, relatives, and work associates. Marketing starts with the quality of a church's ministries, so there is something good to tell. And it goes forward through "satisfied customers" inviting others with whom they have built relationships. National studies verify that new people are much more likely to visit churches recommended by someone they trust.

Viable marketing strategies for your church have two incredibly important components: (1) make the church effective for those who attend and (2) train them how to tell others what they have found. That includes teaching your people to invite, provide on-site welcome and hospitality, and do postvisit follow-up.

Marketing is the way we deliver the Christian gospel to those who need it most.

▪5▪

PURPOSE-DRIVEN ASSIMILATION
How to Increase Visitor Retention

Dale Galloway

Mark McGwire and Sammy Sosa set new home-run records in 1998. They became living examples that the difference between a superstar and an ordinary player in baseball depends on getting more hits at bat. They showed us that if you want to be a major league star, you must put forth every effort to get even 1 additional hit out of every 10 times at bat. An additional 2 or 3 hits per 10 times at bat would make a player spectacular or even a legend.

Try applying these same ratios to your church. To be a healthy, growing church, your visitor retention rate must be improved. Research shows that visitor retention rate is a little less than 1 out of 10 in nongrowing churches. But like a baseball superstar, when a church increases its retention rate to 2 out of 10, it will become a growing church; and 3 or more out of 10, it will be a multiplying church.

The reality is that if your church does not connect and retain people, you lose them out the back door. When that happens, all the efforts and spiritual energy invested to win them is lost. And even though an exciting atmosphere and attractive programs may keep your church's attendance averages up, people who go out the back door may never darken any church's front doors again. The loss is great to the church, but the potential long-term spiritual loss to the one who leaves is disheartening and even frightening.

Give Attention to Seekers and Believers

It becomes significant, then, that a healthy church must assimilate many new people while efficiently serving and retaining

75

present members. Winning new people while losing more established members never builds a healthy church. Assimilation takes work, commitment, and intentional efforts. Savvy and strategies are needed to effectively assimilate new people into the life of your church.

B y assimilation I mean moving people through the development stages of faith into a relational-based identification with a congregation.

Let's be sure we are on the same page with basic definitions. By assimilation I mean moving people through the development stages of faith into a relational-based identification with a congregation. Assimilation is the whole process that begins the first time you meet someone and continues until he or she becomes a responsible Christian involved in church and reaching out to reproduce new converts. The process usually takes a couple of years. This time estimate comes from my experience, based on the fact that I have spent two-thirds of my life trying to lead people to Christ and discipling them through small groups.

In this chapter I want to narrow our discussion pertaining to assimilation to how to keep visitors coming back and how to challenge them to follow and serve Christ.

Correct Your Weaknesses

Think about your church. How effectively do you retain visitors until they become authentic members? And how can you increase the percentage of visitors? Tom, a retailer on the board at New Hope Community Church, was a close friend of mine. He loved to ask about the church: "Dale, how's business?" I would tell him we were doing just fine. I gave him all this positive stuff.

Then he would dampen my enthusiasm with the question, "Now tell me the truth; what's wrong?"

"Nothing is wrong," I'd answer. Then he reminded me, "I never improve my business until I look at what is wrong and fix it." That idea sank in. So I wrote down five areas where the church needed to improve. Interestingly, all five areas had been strengthened when I checked six months later. That improvement happened because we focused, made adjustments, and implemented improvements. The awareness of weakness, as it so often is, was the factor that motivated improvements.

Improvement always starts with an awareness of present weaknesses. Let's make a frank admission that most churches do not do assimilation well. Usually we excuse our own poor retention by saying we are doing as well as others. But that is not a good answer. The haunting question that is tied closely to our Christ-exalting mission as a church, then, is, How do we retain more visitors? Kingdom consequences depend on us.

Consider asking yourself the following: How does the church I serve need to improve assimilation and retention? What strategies can we design to insure that needed improvements happen? How can I make sure better visitor retention rate will take place? What would I be willing to do, or say, or spend to increase retention?

MAKE SURE YOUR SERVICE IS WORTH COMING BACK TO

Exciting worship is a significant key to increasing visitor retention. I call it celebrative worship. By that I propose that every part of a service encourages exaltation of God and contributes to spiritual needs of the individual. True worship must be holy, refreshing, and awe-inspiring—it must make people aware that they are in the presence of God. Everything we do in that worship service must be significant, and we cannot allow it to fall to the level of entertainment or mere performance.

Real worship is a unique encounter with God that people cannot experience anywhere else. Authentic worship helps people meet God among His family. Nothing cheap or shallow is worthy of this holy meeting. The Father seeks worshipers who worship Him in spirit and in truth (John 4:23-24)—that's a sobering expectation given us by our Lord. The opportunities are incredible and awesome.

Here are ways to make your services worth coming back to:
1. Environment—is the atmosphere inviting and accepting?
2. Seeker friendly—does the service speak to needs people feel?

3. Music—is the music inspiring, and does it connect with the people?
4. Time—is time invested in the service well spent, productive, and helpful?
5. Excellence—are all parts of the service done with excellence?
6. Sermon—does the sermon communicate relevant biblical truth?
7. Experience—do the people genuinely experience God's presence?
8. Scripture—does Scripture have high impact?
9. Prayer—is the prayer time well thought out and meaningful?
10. Logistics—are lighting, sound, and visuals pleasing?

One significant conclusion has been forming in me during the last couple of years as I travel among many churches. I marvel to see how God uses various kinds of worship. Many worship styles and religious traditions seem to be used by the Lord to meet people at the point of their need. I honestly do not know what style is most effective, though I have my personal preferences. I realize certain worship practices attract specific target groups. And though I desperately desire worship to be seeker sensitive, that does not mean our services should be believer repulsive.

Stop the Wars

Too much of what we do in worship is culturally relevant but spiritually empty. Too many worship wars, without doing anyone much good, divide the church. Could it be that too much of what seems important is beside the point? Could it be that too much of what we gave up in order to be culturally relevant matters after all? Could it be that substance is more important than style?

I believe the main issue in worship is that people need and want to experience God. With all the secular emphasis on spirituality in books, magazines, and newspapers, it seems obvious that contemporary folks want to know God. If that observation is accurate, and I believe it is, the questions for us must then be how to bring hungry people into the Presence, how to help them genuinely encounter God, and how to teach them to develop a relationship with Him. They want reality in worship. They want to meet God and know it.

CALL VISITORS GUESTS

I strongly recommend that visitors be called guests. A guest is someone special whom you honor and treat with the greatest kindness. Give your guests VIP (Very Important Person) treatment. Scripture offers this VIP principle: "In everything, do to others what you would have them do to you" (Matt. 7:12). This VIP concept simply means we treat others as we want to be treated. They deserve to be treated better than the most effective business down the street treats their best customers.

Put yourself in the place of a visitor to your church. What do they see? How are they treated? What are they likely to feel? And what are their first impressions?

Think like a new person. I used to do that in Portland. On Sundays, I looked out on the parking lot and asked myself, If I were coming here today as a guest, what would I feel? What would I see? What are they going to experience today? Why do they come, anyway?

The way to even better understand these issues is to ask what you would like to experience as a first-time visitor. Try to see things through their eyes. For sure, you would not want to be embarrassed or asked to stand. You would want to be accepted. You would want to be a part of the group. You would want to feel welcome. You would want to be treated as if you mattered. So do your guests.

CALL GREETERS HOSTS, AND INCREASE VISITOR TOUCHES

The next logical step is to give your greeters a title—hosts. A host is one who genuinely cares for the needs of his or her guest. When you host someone in your home or office, you do everything you can to make that one feel important and comfortable.

Hosting a guest implies the start of a relationship. That is much more than saying hello to a visitor. Try to use persons for this important task who have the special gift of hospitality.

The key indicator as to whether a church feels friendly to a visiting guest depends on how many people initiate a conversation with him or her. This skill can be taught to laypeople. The hosts need a passion for making new people feel comfortable. Their task is more than a welcome but the start of a conversation that tells the guests they are important and that in this church somebody would like to know them better.

One sure way to double your visitor retention rate is to double acceptance and friendship.

One sure way to double your visitor retention rate is to double acceptance and friendship. To help guests feel more welcome and to help church people express friendship, intentionally increase the number of personal touches visitors receive. There is a direct ratio between how many touches they receive and whether they return. To state it more specifically, the more touches guests experience, the more apt they are to want to return.

Let's sort out the touches and determine how they can be intentionally planned and multiplied.

Touch 1—Parking lot hosts. For a healthy church, effective hosting starts in the parking lot. When I think about New Hope Community Church's parking lot hosts, I remember Jesus' words, "He that is greatest among you shall be your servant" (Matt. 23:11, KJV).

The reason I think that way about them is because of Oregon weather with its rain and ice storms. Rain or shine, warm or cold, the parking lot hosts were out in the parking lots to extend the first welcome to our guests. Sometimes the hosts would be soaked to the skin and chilled to the bone. Still they were there with big umbrellas, greeting people with a smile and directing them to the church's various facilities. What an impact that team made on guests—their unspoken message came through loud and clear: Someone cares enough about me as a visitor to stand in the rain and cold to welcome me.

At New Hope, the best parking spaces were reserved for guests. So the parking lot hosts always enjoyed directing guests to VIP parking. We saw to it that at New Hope, you simply could not get out of your car without being warmly greeted by someone who believed guests were important. This tremendous ministry of helps was led by a small group of faithful workers who did their work with joy—and it showed.

Touch 2—Foyer hosts. These people host your guests as they come into the buildings, and you need many of them. At New Hope, our foyer hosts showed visitors to a guest table under a huge welcome sign that provided appropriate information for every phase of ministry. First-class, up-to-date literature was always available at that table. The foyer hosts offered to hang up guests' coats. And they provided diagrams and a map to help people find classrooms, rest rooms, nursery, and sanctuary.

If guests were early for the service, these hosts took them to the fellowship center, where they could enjoy a cup of coffee and relax before coming back for the service. This provided another relational opportunity for the guests to be welcomed by our regular attenders.

Foyer hosts must be trained never to ask certain questions. The most obvious no-no question: "Is this your first time here?" In a larger church, people may have been attending for months or even years, and they are insulted with the question.

I will never forget once when I asked a man, "Is this your mother?" and he responded with, "No, it's my wife."

I do not know how many times I caught myself saying something like "It is so good to have you here *for your first-time visit.*" They would sometimes look at me and think, "Poor dumb pastor; I've been coming here for eight months."

Also train foyer hosts to understand the importance of the nursery. If you want to reach young families, you need a well-staffed, professional nursery with adequate, attractive facilities. It must be clean and well run. And the personnel must have been given a rigorous security check. A baby checkout system must also be in place so people who did not bring the children there cannot get them out of the nursery. Church guests want to know the nursery is clean, warm, loving, and secure. Money spent in the nursery is among the best investments you can make in ministry. The best nursery workers are those who give lots of love but project professional conduct and positive attitudes. But new people won't know about your nursery unless the hosts tell them.

In my experience, volunteer nursery workers do not work well. The main reason is that mothers have been involved with children all week. So when they come to church, they do not want to take care of babies. These mothers are often the women who most need the worship service.

Of course, you can supplement your nursery staff with volunteers, but we thought it was money well spent to hire people who were willing to be trained, who made a good appearance, and who provided a positive impression to parents. This emphasis of good nursery programs paid off over the years because many young families were attracted to our church through the nursery personnel and facilities.

Touch 3—Hosting ushers. You want to strategically place ushers at the sanctuary entrance and throughout the sanctuary. Train ushers to be considerate and positive. Too many ushers look sour, gruff, and disinterested. Others stand over in a corner talking while completely ignoring the persons you want them to help. Ushers, like other volunteers, tend to forget their opportunities and responsibilities unless they are periodically retrained.

Your head usher needs to be chosen carefully and trained fully in what you are trying to do so he can communicate the church's mission over and over again to those who serve with him in this assignment. Almost nothing is more important to visitor retention than to have smiling, friendly, helpful ushers. Train them to remember that first impressions are lasting impressions.

Touch 4—Everyone becomes a host. Have a time in the worship service where people greet one another warmly. This practice was called "passing the peace" in earlier periods of church history, a time when worshipers greeted each other by saying, "May the peace of God be with you." This effort puts everyone at ease so no one feels embarrassed or singled out. It is a way of connecting guests with other people. Push your congregation to continually be thinking of ways to make people feel accepted and affirmed. Make a big deal of welcoming everyone, especially new people.

Touch 5—Welcome people from the pulpit. I like to give visitors a small gift, usually a book. In this process, I never had guests stand up or be singled out. I simply said, "We are glad to have many guests with us today, and a host near you is ready to present you with a gift if you will lift your hand." Then we sometimes gave visitors a big applause.

At this time in the service, we also tell guests about our hospitality room, where they are invited to go following the service. This welcome from the pulpit is another way to break through barriers for new people. Though it may not seem important to pastors, people really enjoy being welcomed by the most visible leader of the church.

It is important to remember that a spirit of genuine love always breaks through even the most impossible barriers of limited facility, culture, or location.

Touch 6—Hospitality room. We had a hospitality room right off the foyer. Every Sunday after service, we served cookies and punch there. That is a great way to welcome people, to learn their names and occupations.

During the service, we often told the entire congregation about the hospitality room—its purpose and location. Then we would say to guests, "We would be pleased to meet you in the hospitality room following the service." Be sure to tell them that anyone in the congregation can help them find the place because everyone has been there at least once when first attending this church.

Tell them if they have questions about the church, someone will be there to give them answers and explain the church's ministries. The map they received earlier will help them locate the hospitality room.

This hospitality area must be staffed by warm, friendly, knowledgeable individuals who communicate well. They must be trained to fully understand the ministry of the church and to find the answer if a guest has a question they cannot answer. Try to be sure that at least one staff person is in the hospitality room following every service so he or she can help make the connection.

I always tried to drop in myself. It is a wonderful way for a senior pastor to get acquainted with people. Other staff pastors dropped by too. After briefly greeting guests, I usually returned to the main door to greet everyone.

Those who serve as hosts in the hospitality room always urge guests to attend the pastor's welcome class. A guest's interest in that class often reflects their level of interest in the church. As the hospitality touch takes place, refreshments are served. Questions are answered. Positive conversations are exchanged. And visitors feel valued and welcomed.

Touch 7—Coffee host. Our first sanctuary was just down the hall from where we built our new sanctuary. When we built our new building, we did not realize how useful it would be to have these facilities so close together. But in the old sanctuary, which became a multipurpose room, we placed round tables and served lots of coffee and doughnuts before and after services. It was a gathering place for guests and regular attenders. As we sat around round tables, we conversed naturally and formed new connections.

Notice the difference between the coffee room and the hospitality room. The hospitality room is used primarily for making contact with first-time guests. The coffee room is for everyone who wants to use it.

Touch 8—After-service hosting. This involves being sure friendly people are stationed throughout the building and especially at the doors to shake hands with guests and regular attenders as they leave. The greeting should be natural and positive—something like "We're glad you came today" or "God bless you" or "Please come again" or "Have a wonderful day."

After-service hosting is among the most important factors that determine whether people come back.

Many churches do a good job of hosting guests before the service, but after the service these connections break down. In many places, it seems everyone wants to run for the exit. Research tells us, however, that after-service hosting is among the most important factors that determine whether people come back.

Make it impossible for anyone to leave your church without being greeted by at least 5 to 10 people. Remember, the goal is to touch people as often as you can so they will come again. The idea of commissioning everyone to host guests does not depend on the size of your church; any church can do it and do it well. It is a spirit and a commitment and a strategy that makes it work. Since many people are shy or afraid to get to know others naturally, they must be trained and reminded often to welcome others in the name of Jesus.

Touch 9—Telecare phone ministry. Telecare is a phone-based contact system done by well-trained people who call during prime times in the evenings and on Saturday. They call recent guests as well as regular attenders. They contact guests within 24-48 hours. They contact the whole constituency of our church about every six to eight weeks.

To guests, their message goes like this: "We're so glad to have you attend our church. Is there any information you'd like to have? We would love to have you come again. If you're looking for a church home, we recommend that you attend the pastor's welcome class. The class would give you an opportunity to learn more about our church and to personally meet the pastor."

To regular attenders, they say: "My name is ———, and I am calling for Pastor ———. Any information you need to know about the church? Do you have needs we can pray for? Is there anything you'd like us to communicate to the pastor—any kind of special spiritual need in your life? Are you enjoying your small group?"

These callers pray for expressed needs on the phone. Then they write down the information received during the phone call and place it in the lay pastor's mailbox.

In the first eight years of our telecare ministry, volunteers prayed more than 200,000 prayers. That's a lot of important ministry that keeps people spiritually connected to the church.

From the church, all communication must make people feel that what happens to them matters to us. Telecare is an effective way to help close the back door of the church.

Touch 10—Personal letter. A welcome letter from the senior pastor is sent first thing Monday morning to new guests.

Since this letter will likely be a computer-generated one, you should work hard to write a concise, high-impact, friendly, attractive follow-up letter. Then check out that letter periodically to be sure it says precisely what you want to say to newcomers. Be sure to sign the letters personally.

In this touch, like many others, an invitation to the pastor's welcome class is given and the purpose of the class explained. The invitation can be personalized by your saying, "I look forward to meeting you at the pastor's class."

Touch 11—Small-group involvement. Every guest card is given to a small-group leader, who phones to welcome the guest to church and to invite him or her to participate in a small group. The small-group leader actually becomes a lay pastor to this person. That's why it is so important to connect small-group leaders with guests. Notice how quickly the sense of welcome, belonging, and connecting begin to take place through the small-group leader—almost immediately.

As churches grow, they often lose the personal touch, have no effective way to deliver genuine pastoral care, and offer no strategy for people to make new friends at church. But small groups, when properly designed and implemented, solve all these needs for you and your church's guests.

STRANGE REALITY—PEOPLE WANT TO BELONG, BUT THEY RESIST

Ask yourself and others what visitors desire when they attend your church for the first time. Usually they are asking themselves subconsciously, "Is there someone here like me?" They want to know if there is anyone with whom they can identify. If they can meet or even imagine that someone there might like them, they will generally come back. Of course, most guests do not ask themselves these questions out loud, but that is what is often going on inside them.

Strangely enough, many people want to belong but resist belonging. Church leaders, both clergy and lay, need to understand this confusing reality. To serve people well, a church must build these factors into their follow-up procedures. How do we translate such an awareness into action?

When I started New Hope Community Church, there were

years when I personally called on every guest. Guess what I discovered in those contacts: About half the new people were glad I called, but the other half were not sure. Some want to be contacted, while others want to be left alone. It is a puzzling paradox.

At the drive-in church, some would sit in their cars week after week and make no move for friendship. Still they kept coming. But then we had weeks when people really responded when we said, "We have refreshments up at the front here, and we would like for you to get out of your car and come down so we can get acquainted."

WHAT DO PEOPLE WANT FROM A CHURCH?

One of the most important things people want is to feel needed. That is why we cannot expect them to attend for years before asking them to do anything. If we do, they go out the back door very quickly. The trick is to ask them to do what they can do, what they are interested in doing, and what the church needs for them to do.

People overlook lots of faults and mistakes if they know they are loved.

People want to give and receive love, even when they do not know how to do it. There is an important reality here that every pastor needs to recognize. People overlook lots of faults and mistakes if they know they are loved. Loving people stands at the heart of the Christian gospel.

All people need hope. Many feel beaten down by circumstances and disappointed by broken dreams. Help them believe in themselves. Inspire them to become more than they think they can become. Teach them to deal with their sins and the continuing consequences. If you help people find salvation, hope, and new beginnings, you will have more people attending your church than you can handle.

People desire to feel important and find healing for their guilt and shame. They are hungry for what the church has to offer. This means the church must specialize in its uniqueness and must make use of its supernatural power. I find Bob Blass's list of five things people want from a church very useful:

1. Friendliness and warmth
2. Experience God
3. Ministry for children
4. An adult program
5. The church building itself

Make access convenient. You cannot travel on I-205 in Portland without seeing New Hope Community Church. We had high visibility, so everyone knew where we were. But accessibility was difficult. The exit off the freeway turned into a two-lane highway, so it was difficult to move cars out after a service. Now the church is working on that problem, and they will eventually have much better access, but it will take several years. The questions about property are visibility, accessibility, adequacy, and up-keep. The facility must help fulfill the mission of the church.

HOW TO DO EFFECTIVE FOLLOW-UP

The two most pressing issues concerning follow-up are (1) how to get names and addresses and (2) how to quickly follow up after guests visit your church.

You want to keep building your prospect list. You want to pray over that prospect list. You want to work it effectively. And you must keep enlarging that list. Whose names should be on your prospect list? It is people you are working to bring into your church.

Never forget the following statistic: Effective immediate follow-up increases visitors' return rate by 25 percent. That means that next to the multiple-touch concept, follow-up is the most effective way to grow a healthy church. Touch and follow-up work together. The question then is, How do we follow up after we have put all the touches in place? The answer is the quicker the better. Follow-up must be done according to some efficient systematic plan that communicates a personal interest.

Follow-up starts with an effective communication card attendees fill out during worship. You must develop a communication card where everyone records his or her attendance every Sunday. Do not expect guests to complete the cards unless they see regular attenders doing it.

In some fashion, every attender in every service has to receive a communication card. Some churches put them in bulletins. Some use tear-off sheets on bulletins. And others place them in the pew card racks. But every person must receive a card and be urged to fill out the card.

Then at an appropriate point in the service, the pastor says, "We would like for everyone to take a communication card in hand. Let's communicate. We are happy you are here today, and we want a record of your attendance. Please indicate on the card if you are a first-, second-, or third-time guest with us. On the back of the card, please list your prayer requests so we can pray for those needs."

Cynics among guests always wonder, of course, how the card will be used. For that reason, we tell people up front that information on the card will be used for church purposes only. We never allow anyone outside the church to use the mailing list. We faithfully honor that commitment. We tell them if they check the appropriate box, we will put them on the mailing list to receive information about coming events at New Hope Community Church.

As soon as the cards are received, if possible even during the service, we take them to our computer center, where the information is entered in the computer. Then the card is passed to a small-group leader who is committed to following up as soon as possible.

Consider these effective follow-up principles:

Follow-Up Principle 1—The Time Principle

Contact all guests within 48 hours of their visit. People have such busy schedules, they do not appreciate or expect a home visit, but they will usually welcome a properly designed phone call.

Follow-Up Principle 2—Goal Is to Get Visitor to Return

Back to the basic idea at the beginning of this chapter: If you can get 2 or 3 guests in 10 to return, you can grow a church. If you get 1 in 10, you will only maintain your attendance. Every touch and every follow-up effort must be planned to move people from guests to regular attenders and to increase the return rate of visitors. Get the goal in focus for everyone who has any part in the touch and follow-up efforts. Helping guests return the second, third, or fourth time brings them closer and closer to making a decision for Christ and becoming an active member of the church.

Follow-Up Principle 3—Double Impact

The visitor return rate doubles when laypersons follow up on guests. When people visit a church, they expect to hear from the pastor or ministerial staff. But a follow-up visit or phone call from a layperson is flattering and novel, maybe even surprising. Guests begin to think New Hope Community Church must be a great church if laypersons believe in it so much. Then, too, laypersons can brag on the pastor and the ministry of the church without being suspected of being a prejudiced paid witness.

I especially love Elton Trueblood's pithy sentence, "Laypeople are not the passengers of a ship, but members of the crew." Great churches cannot be built without thoughtful, intentional, and efficient involvement of laypersons. And they have incredibly effective outcomes in follow-up efforts.

Follow-Up Principle 4—Entry Path

Effective follow-up must open opportunities for people to become involved. This is a bit tricky, because some people are eager to get involved quickly, while others have a wait-and-see attitude. So the idea is to open the door but not force anyone to walk through it.

I was always amazed at who showed up for a valentine dinner or a men's retreat. Such interest is a positive sign that they are serious about your church. But newcomers cannot express that interest if they do not know about the events or do not know someone who will be there. The idea is to inform and welcome without smothering them.

The secret is to intentionally create entry paths and to be sure those paths are communicated to new people. Often a personal invitation to an event is almost as effective as their actual attendance. People need to be aware of entry level paths to fellowship and service while not feeling pressured to move into church life faster than they wish.

Follow-Up Principle 5—The Connection Necessity

If new people are not connected with others, you lose them. One of the ways we made this connection at New Hope was to provide ministries that touched people at the point of some important felt need. We offered ministries like substance addiction recovery groups, divorce recovery groups, and parental skill groups.

Another way was to get them connected with small groups. We expected group leaders to follow up, and they did. Remember, the same satisfactions you experienced when you served as pastor of a small church are also available to a leader of a small group. This creates enormous motivation for lay leaders if you highlight it for them to see.

Quick response to issues people checked on their communication cards is another important way to connect with people. If they checked an item on the guest welcome card, they have a right to expect a response. The longer a response takes, the less interest you are likely to find.

Keep checking these connections to be sure they are being made. Follow-up systems have a tendency to break down if the senior pastor does not keep pushing to make them effective. The issue is not to check on volunteers, but to increase the return rate to 2 or 3 in 10, as we discussed at the start of this chapter.

Follow-Up Principle 6—Allow Freedom to Determine Intensity

This principle simply means that your church is ready to respond whenever a guest takes a step toward you. The idea—when they take a step forward, you take a step to meet them halfway. This principle means you give people freedom to be left alone if that is what they want, but if they want to be known, you get to know them. You must recognize that people are at different places in their willingness to go public about their interest in your church. Win Arn, the church growth specialist, reminds us, "Ministry in the purest and simplest form is love. Ministry is, in fact, doing love!" And such love allows people to move into church involvement and spiritual development at their own pace.

Follow-Up Principle 7—Friendship Factor

Everyone needs more friends, and many people who come

to church are seeking friends. Others come with friends and stay because of their friends.

I am quite sure most churches have not scratched the surface in winning people in the friend/relative networks of their members. The literature informs us that everyone has 10 to 15 relationships outside the church—neighbors, workmates, friends, and relatives. The number is fairly constant for people who attend growing churches, those who attend stagnated churches, or those who attend no church.

Growing churches teach members how to invite and evangelize the people in their friendship network. Nongrowing churches seldom use those networks. The awareness of those networks needs to be explained to church members. The importance of evangelizing these networks must be understood by small groups and their leaders. And they need to be taught how to use them.

Follow-Up Principle 8—Tracking

To keep people coming, track their attendance patterns and their own understanding of what those patterns mean. That's why the communication card asks people to indicate whether they are first-, second-, or third-time guests or regular attenders. It is significant to know how guests view these relationships.

When they checked the card as a regular attender, you knew they had decided to be part of the church. That's the time to really work hard to get them involved in the pastor's welcome class. Up until now, they have been made aware of the class and welcomed to it. But when they mark "regular attender," you must get much more serious about telling them the church's story, seeking to win them to Christ, and urging them to join the church.

That designation—"regular attender"—is a significant milestone in the assimilation process; don't miss this golden opportunity.

How to Develop and Use the Pastor's Welcome Class

Too many churches fail to invite people to such a class until they have been born again and are faithful church attenders. But when I visited a Wednesday night class at Crystal Cathedral during one of Dr. Robert Schuller's pastors' conferences, I discovered a new and useful paradigm.

The pastor's welcome class there was led by one of Schuller's assistants. In the middle of the first class, the leader presented the plan of salvation and urged people to receive Christ; and they did.

The pastor's welcome class provides a golden opportunity for evangelism—use it. Here's how I did it. After getting acquainted with people, I started the class with two questions: (1) What brought you to New Hope Community Church? and (2) Why did you come back? Their answers told me so much about our church—what we were doing right and what needed to be improved. George Hunter is right: "Feedback is the breakfast of champions." This is feedback at its best. New people can tell you so much you need to know about your church, but you have to ask them.

Another benefit of feedback from those questions is that it helped convince persons attending the class who had doubts about getting involved. Their affirming answers sold others on New Hope. In a short time frame, persons attending this class underscored the many strengths of the church, and it became obvious then that everyone should want to be a vital part of it.

On a regular basis, 60 percent of those attending made commitments to Christ in that class. When we left Portland, the church had 6,400 members, and the pastor's welcome class was one of the main ways we won people to Christ.

Let's be sure we understand the unique advantages of the pastor's welcome class:

1. It provides entry points to the church.
2. It gives opportunity for a person to make a commitment to Christ.
3. It helps people connect to the church as the Body of Christ.
4. It encourages people to get involved in ministries and relate to a small group.
5. It provides a way to assess how assimilation is going.
6. It helps the pastor share the vision, doctrines, and ministry of the church.

7. It allows people to discover their spiritual gifts and introduces them to ministry opportunities.

MONITOR YOUR ASSIMILATION SYSTEMS

When done in love, all these follow-up efforts will increase your retention rate. But you will need to constantly monitor the progress. Monitor to see that everyone is doing his or her job, and evaluate to see if you are getting the desired results.

I strongly recommend that you create your own assimilation system, but use some of the ideas I have explained in this chapter. See to it that volunteers are giving attention to the details of the plan; most plans start to unravel when even one component is failing.

Never assume the assimilation system is working effectively. Any assimilation system you do not monitor, inspect, and get feedback from will go downhill. Adjusting and improving your assimilation system is always desirable and needed.

Though the assimilation task is never completely finished, the results are wonderful and eternal. For example, a Lutheran church near Chicago called me to report the telecare phone ministry worked for them after they adjusted it to their situation. They discovered they were losing a good percentage of people within two years after they joined the church. So they doubled up on the number of times they contacted those people as compared to the frequency of phoning the general constituency. They said, "By increasing those contacts, we raised the percentage of people who were sticking with us after that first year."

Here's the concept. Design a system that will work for you, and then work it.

Always remember, the assimilation goal is to win 2 or 3 more persons out of every 10 who visit your church. Though I have shared a detailed system here, it is more than a mere system. It is a new way of doing church.

Our efforts at New Hope were an attempt to keep the whole church focused on winning and assimilating new people. I urge you to give thoughtful attention to assimilation details. Keep monitoring your system. Keep improving your strategies. Keep training your people.

And the Father will help you win and keep more people.

▪ 6 ▪

MAKING SENSE OF YOUR COMMUNITY'S CULTURE

Lessons from Jesus, Paul, and Patrick

George Hunter III

Jesus helps us understand the range of human responses to the gospel with the parable of the soils. He taught us that the harvest potential built into the Word of God never changes. But the conditions of the soil and our cultivation of the soil influence the size of the harvest.

Painting in bold strokes, in this famous parable Jesus talked about four different populations. The evil one steals the seed scattered upon trampled ground, so it never germinates. Seed sown on rocky soil produces tender plants that wither in the hot sun. Seed sown on thorny soil gets choked by the weeds of anxiety and deception. But when sown on good soil, the Word of God produces a crop that multiplies 30, 60, or even 100 times. The message is clear: Seek to understand the soil, and use that knowledge to advance the gospel.

You may recall that Paul, as his ministry is described in the Book of Acts and reflected in his letters to the churches in specific cities, consistently models the need to understand a community's population and a society's values. Secular scholars who study the ancient world now regard Paul's letters as primary sources for understanding the populations and cultures of those ancient cities. Paul was an expert at understanding receptivity for the gospel. His understanding shows up often in his writings.

Meet Patrick—a Saint Who Impacted a Culture

A long time ago, around A.D. 400, a 16-year-old boy was being raised in the northwest section of what is now England. He was a romanized Briton. Latin had become his family's first language, though he might have known some of the British-Celtic language of the servants. His name was Patricius, that is, Patrick. He was a nominal member of the church. Though he had been thoroughly immersed in the catechism as a child, he tells us later that he did not really believe it. He and his young friends enjoyed making fun of the clergy. He admits that he lived close to the wild side.

One day around the year 400, a marauding band of pirates swept through the section of England where Patrick lived, apprehending all the young men they could find. They herded their human cargo onto a ship, sailed for what is now Ireland, and sold them into slavery. Patricius was purchased by a Celtic tribal leader whose name was Miliuk. Miliuk took him back to his own tribe, where Patrick was put to work herding cattle as a slave.

Three things happened in this period of Patrick's life that eventually changed the course of Western history.

First, he found God. Out in the wilderness with the cattle for days on end, through the winds, the seasons, the birdsongs, and the beauty of sunrises and sunsets, he was profoundly impacted by what theologians call "natural revelation." He experienced the presence of God in nature. He connected this Presence with the God he learned about in the catechism. He began pray-

A voice directed him to awaken early before daybreak the next morning and start walking in a certain direction.

ing. In time, he was praying a hundred times a day and almost as many times at night. Sometimes he would fall asleep praying. Patrick became devout, and the change became obvious to his captors.

Second, in the lengthy period in which he was enslaved, he learned the language, culture, and ways of his captors. Indeed, he learned their language and culture from the underside—where avoiding a beating might depend on how well he understood his owners.

Third, to his astonishment, he came to love his captors. In time, he so much identified with them that he counted himself as one of them, more than he counted himself as a romanized Briton.

One night, sleeping close to the cattle out in the wilderness, after working as a slave for six years, Patrick had a dream. A voice directed him to awaken early before daybreak the next morning and start walking in a certain direction. He was to walk as long as necessary. He was promised a ship would be waiting to take him to freedom.

He awakened early the next morning, gathered his gear, and started walking. Miraculously, he was not detected by the people of any Celtic tribe as he walked to the seashore, which may have taken several days. As a result, he felt protected. He believed himself to be under the sheltering providence of God. He arrived at the seashore, saw the ship, and negotiated his way on board.

The next 25 years of his life, the period of which we have only fragments of information, probably took him to Gaul. He likely spent some time in Rome. He eventually wound up in England. We know he acquired a theological education somewhere along the way, and in England he became a faithful parish priest.

One night at the age of 48, Patrick had another dream. An angel named Victor approached him in this dream with a stack of letters from people Patrick had known during his captivity as a young man. He opened a letter and read this message: "O, holy boy, come walk among us again." When he awakened the next morning, he vividly recalled the dream and interpreted it to be his Macedonian call. He believed himself directed by God to take the gospel to the Irish.

Patrick shared this "called" experience with two bishops in that region of England, and they bought it. Apparently Pope Celestine I bought it as well. Within months, this priest Patrick was ordained to be the apostolic bishop to the Irish.

This was an incredibly historic decision because the Irish

were barbarians in the eyes of the Roman Empire. Throughout the expansion of Roman Christianity in Europe, it had been assumed that a person had to be at least somewhat civilized by Rome's standards in order to become a Christian. For this reason, there had never been a systematic missionary effort to the Franks, Goths, Visigoths, Vandals, or Celtic tribes—all these groups were regarded as unreachable barbarians.

Why did Rome regard the Irish as barbarians? The Romans assumed that anybody who was not an enculturated, Latin-speaking Roman was suspect. Then, too, the Irish could not read or write and were not interested in learning. Theirs was an oral culture with remarkable memories. But Rome assumed literacy was indispensable to being civilized. Roman culture also greatly prized emotional control. They had heard that the Irish practiced *no* emotional control. So, whether the Irish experienced grief, lust, joy, or sadness, their emotional expression was *unrestrained*. Rome also considered the Irish barbarians because their primal religion of the Druids practiced human sacrifice—which did not square with Roman understanding of civilization! Finally, in warfare, the Irish and other Celts would sometimes fight naked, wearing nothing but a belt around their necks, a belt around their arms, and sandals on their feet. The opposing Roman army would have remembered their appearance.

So the word got out that in regard to language, learning, emotional control, primal religion, and fighting practices, the Irish were barbarians. It was assumed, by definition, that barbarians were incapable of becoming genuine Christians.

Nevertheless, Patrick had been reflecting for nearly a quarter century on how barbarian people *could* be reached. So in 432, Patrick and a small entourage of priests, nuns, and seminarians set out for Ireland, where he spent the rest of his life. Though he was already past the life expectancy of a man in the fifth century, he lived to the age of 70.

By the time of his death, what did he have to show for his efforts? It appears that about 40 of the 150 Celtic tribes of Ireland had been substantially evangelized before Patrick died. In the next two generations, his successors took the gospel to virtually all the remaining Celtic tribes of Ireland.

In 563 the Irish believers commissioned an apostolic leader named Columba to set sail for an island off the coast of Scotland called Iona to take the gospel to another Celtic barbarian people called the Picts. Within three generations, both the northern Picts and the southern Picts had been substantially reached.

In 633 Iona commissioned a great leader named Aidan to establish another monastic community and mission station on Lindisfarne, off the coast of northeast England, which would be used as a mission base for reaching the Anglo-Saxons, that in the previous century overwhelmed both north and central England. Within three generations, the Anglo-Saxons had become substantially evangelized.

In this same time period, the Irish sent another towering figure named Columbanus, who with an entourage of about a dozen people set out for the continent of Europe. They established many monastic communities, which planted many more churches. As a result, within a couple hundred years, most of the barbarian populations that had overwhelmed Europe had been introduced to Christ. This Christianizing effort effectively lifted the Dark Ages and ushered in the Holy Roman Empire. As one writer of history put it, "That is how the Irish saved civilization."

What were the keys? How were they able to reach populations that the established church assumed could not be reached?

I attempt to uncover a number of factors that work synergistically to achieve this great mission to the European barbarians in my book *The Celtic Way of Evangelism.* I am underscoring only one point now.

There is no shortcut to understanding people.

Patrick, his successors—Columba, Aidan, and Columbanus—and their entourages paid the price to *understand* the target population. They understood them so well that the target population felt understood. Their target audiences reasoned that if Christians understand us, then maybe their God understands us. In their primal religions, they assumed that the high God does not know us or care about us and is not accessible.

Patrick, Aidan, and the others stand as eternal witnesses to any church that wants to become a contagious movement. There is no shortcut to understanding people. And when you truly understand them, you will often understand how to reach them. Then you will discover they are receptive to you and your God as they sense you understand them.

Such thorough understanding is the historical and theological rationale for what we call community analysis—which is an intentional and effective expression of the incarnational ministry.

EXAMPLE OF WESLEY

Most great Christian leaders have been astute students of their target populations. Consider the example of John Wesley. As a common practice, Wesley wrote in his journal almost every night. If you work through Wesley's journals, you understand he recorded what he was learning about his target audience as he was traveling, preaching, observing, listening in on class meetings, interviewing people, and listening in town squares. We have reason to believe that when he set out on another itinerary, he would reread his journal entries of the previous years to track the trends among the populations of Newcastle, Bristol, or wherever.

Consequently, Wesley's journal stands even now, among other things, as a rather sophisticated longitudinal study of the people who lived in more than 100 towns and cities on his regular beat.

COMMUNITY ANALYSIS INFORMS MINISTRY

Effective ministry is the primary purpose of community analysis. Its ultimate objective is to understand people to the point they realize they are understood. So the tools—like historical analysis, demographics, and cultural analysis—are a means to effectively communicate the gospel. It leads us to consider how to understand a target group and why.

Gain Historical Perspective

Let's assume you become pastor to the only church of your denomination in a growing county seat town made up of 70 percent pre-Christian people. Part of your challenge is to understand the history of the people in that community. Where did they come from? How old is the town? What brought people to this place? You want to understand migration patterns, ethnic roots, demographic trends, previous history, economic patterns, schools, and the media. Try to identify enduring heroes of the people.

There are certain sources you already know about, like the U.S. census, that you can access. Sometimes you can acquire photocopies of the marketing data from Sears or McDonald's. City planners, school superintendents, and chambers of commerce have also been tracking the community, its trends, and needs of the people. Often the school superintendent can tell you more about the conditions of pre-Christian family units than anyone else. Often local histories have been published and are available at the public library. There are always reflective old-timers who can explain what happened when and what it meant to people.

Raymond Bakke, the well-known urban specialist, reminds us there are always pastors who have long experience in this community to help us discover the details of the community. Bakke tells how, when he moved to a new church in Chicago, he went to veteran pastors in that community and asked one question: What's the most important thing you have learned about ministry in this community? He also talked to shopkeepers and police personnel who had known the community for years. All these persons helped him develop a profile of the unreached populations of that section of Chicago.

Study Demographic Details

Acquire demographic data to help you make sense of your community today. Ask the question, "What do I need to know?"

Rick Warren, in *The Purpose-Driven Church,* suggests that we gather only focused data. He warns against overdoing demographic research: "You can waste a lot of time collecting facts and information about your community that won't make any real difference to your church. . . . There are only a handful of relevant demographic facts that you need to discover about the people in your community." He considers the most important factors in targeting a community for evangelism to be:

Age—How many are in each age-group?

Marital status—How many are single adults? How many are married couples?

Income—What is both the median and the average household income?

Education—What is the education level of the community?

Occupation—What types of jobs are predominant? (163 ff.).

Let me suggest that in many contexts, you may want to know several additional factors:

Ethnicity

Distinct subculture and lifestyle groups

Population density, distribution, recent changes, future projections

Primary concerns and stress conditions

Receptivity to faith, preferences in church style and programming

The good news: You don't have to gather all this data yourself. PRECEPT (1-800-442-6277) can do it for you for a modest price.

Discover Community Values

Values, by definition, are what the people assume to be good and evil. Beliefs are what people assume to be true or false.

For example, think about a woman who has the flu. Depending on the culture or subculture, you will find different explanations for her illness. In some cultures, she assumes she has a germ or virus. But in other cultures, she might assume that her sickness came from bad luck, or an evil spirit, or emotional stress, or a poisoned relationship, or a curse someone had put on her.

The sources for understanding cultural anthropology are local documents, newspapers, and especially the 10 percent of the population who are self-aware and articulate enough to serve as indigenous informants to help you understand what drives their people.

There are various other ways of locating a group's characteristic beliefs and values. The material is an adaptation from John Condon and Fathi S. Yousef's book *An Introduction to Intercultural Communication*. In his categories for exegeting a culture on the following grid, there are assumptions about human nature, relationship between people and nature, and the cosmos. As you work with this material, you will discover that all cultures fall predominantly in one of three columns. In any culture, you will find individuals who fit into all three places, but the preponderance of people in any population will fall in one column.

VALUES

Individualistic	Group	Collectivistic
Youth	The middle years	Old age
Democratic	Authority-centered	Authoritarian
High mobility	Phasic mobility	Low mobility
Live in many groups, brief identification, group subordinate to individual	Balance	Live in few groups, prolonged identification, individual subordinate to group
Informality	Selective formality	Pervasive formality

Let's consider these categories: Notice that the predominant values of Anglo-American culture is on the left side of the triad. For instance, in the U.S.A., we tend toward individualism. Each person has his or her own identity and place in society. Everybody has one vote. Majority rules. We regard ourselves as a nation of individuals.

Over on the right side you find a list of values and beliefs representative of a collectivist culture. Japan is an example where people conform and identify with their primary group. If you met persons from Japan before the urbanization of that country, they would identify themselves in terms of their village or town. Today we find this pattern has been translated to the companies for which they work. And in Japanese culture, the desirable pattern is to remain in the employment of the same company for a lifetime. The company has now replaced the village. So when you meet Japanese people, they usually identify themselves by the company they work for.

In the middle list, you find the group-oriented culture where each person is defined by a social category—like socioeconomic, ancestry, prestige, class. England and Hungary are good examples.

In the next set of categories, you will recognize that the United States is a youth-valuing culture. This is reflected on television and in advertisements. Youth is associated with the vigor and idealism that are also valued in American society. On the other side are the cultures like China who value old age. In those societies, the elders are recognized as possessing knowledge, experience, and wisdom. Therefore, the culture grants them authority to make decisions for the young, even whom to marry. Some cultures especially value the middle years. Indeed nomadic societies of hunters and gatherers may leave behind to die the old who cannot keep up.

In terms of power distribution, the United States tends to be a democratic society. The person in charge is expected to function collaboratively, assimilate everyone's opinion and judgment, and then act according to the will of the social group that elected him or her. On the extreme right column are societies where the person with authority makes the decisions and others obey without question. And in the middle are authority-centered cultures, where authority resides not in a person, or in the whole of a social unit, but in a set of traditions, beliefs, laws, or customs.

Some societies, cultures, and subcultures are highly mobile. For instance, one out of five families still moves each year in the United States. Students go off to college. Youth leave home to make a life for themselves. Other countries value low mobility, even some fairly cosmopolitan societies like Switzerland. In Switzerland, it is almost impossible for people like you and me to become citizens. A person has to live in a town for 15 years before he or she can become a citizen of that town—and even longer to become a citizen of the country. Both their laws and their culture discourage mobility. Some other societies feature phasic mobility, what might also be called a boomerang mobility. In these cultures, a person leaves for college or for the city to work, but it is assumed he or she will come back often, retire as early as possible, and spend the rest of life with his or her people.

In American culture, we tend to belong to many groups, have a brief identification with most of them, and the group is subordinate to the individual. For instance, I am a member of the Speech Communication Association, the American Management Association, the Academy for Evangelism, the American Society for Church Growth, the American Automobile Association, the PTA, and World Gym. Most of these groups would not miss me if I left, moved, or died.

For example, I was a member of Lexington Athletic Club. Then my mom had a stroke and moved into a nursing home. It was inconvenient to get a workout in one part of the city and then go to see her in a different part of the city. So I left Lexington Athletic Club and joined World Gym, which is only a couple of blocks away from where my mother now lives. As I signed out of the Lexington Athletic Club after eight or nine years of membership, the person in charge said, "You've been a good member, George." That was it.

Some societies are just the opposite; a person lives in only a few groups, has prolonged identification with those groups, and the individual is subordinate to the group. Generally, you are born to such a group, like the warrior class within the tribe. Other cultures have a kind of balance in which the individual is in some groups for life but others are optional or transitional.

One of the most predictable trends in effective churches in the U.S. is the casualization of Christianity.

There are countries on the formality/informality scale that are vastly different from each other. Those on the right are characterized by pervasive formality, like Chinese, Japanese, and Arabic cultures. Though they differ from each other in many ways, they have in common the significance of titles, honorifics, and formal codes of conduct. In such a society, communication becomes predictable, and there are few, if any, surprises. Over on the American side, we tend toward extreme informality and tend to think formal codes of conduct get in the way of authentic communication. We tend to consider formality as a mask, pretentious, or sissylike. So one of the most predictable trends in effective churches in the U.S. is the casualization of Christianity.

Other societies practice selective formality, like at a wedding or a funeral, but they may be informal much of the time.

Obviously, there are many other guidelines for discovering the target population's values, but the person who wins secularists must understand the values categories.

Understand Community Beliefs

Now consider Condon's spectrum for exegeting the beliefs of a culture.

Some cultures, like ours, assume that human beings are basically rational (or should be). There is an emphasis in such societies on formal education and the values that came from the Enlightenment. (This is changing increasingly as we enter postmodernity.) By contrast, some other societies are more intuitive than rational in their understanding of human nature. They believe education is not intended to pour information into a person's mind so much as to elicit or awaken what people already know deep down. Many of these societies assume that women are more intuitive than men.

BELIEFS

Humans are:	Rational	Intuitive	Irrational
Humans are:	Good	Good-evil mixture	Evil
Life is:	Mostly happy	An inextricable bond of happiness and sadness	Mostly sadness
People can:	Change, grow, learn	Some change	Unchanging, immutable
Humans:	Dominate nature	Live in harmony	Nature dominates
The world is:	Mechanistic	Spiritual	Organic
Live oriented to:	Future	Present	Past
Life goals:	Physical, material	Intellectual	Spiritual
The cosmic order is:	Comprehensible	Faith and reason	Mysterious and unknowable

Now regarding beliefs, there are societies that believe that human nature is intrinsically good. If people have a problem, it's because of their environment. Other societies see human beings as intrinsically evil. And still others see human nature as a complex mixture of good and evil.

In our society, books and stories are supposed to have a happy ending.

Various societies have contrasting beliefs about what we can expect in this life. In some, life is mostly happy, or at least, that's the goal. In the U.S. we believe, according to our founding documents, in life, liberty, and the pursuit of happiness. In our society, books and stories are supposed to have a happy ending; many Americans feel tricked or even violated if it does not turn out that way. For other societies, the human condition is characterized mostly by sadness. Indian culture and some other Asian cultures regard life as a veil of tears until one escapes life into Nirvana and is absorbed into Brahma. In a third kind of culture, life is an unpredictable blend of happiness and sadness.

In regard to the changeability of human nature, some societies believe that people can change, learn, and grow. Others regard human nature as unchangeable. Even if change were possible, it might not be desirable because such cultures would view change as a threat. Some family units in our society are like this, so when someone in the home experiences conversion, others in the family, often the masculine head of the family, feel threatened to the core.

Like American culture, some other societies believe that human beings are destined to dominate nature. This assumption is mirrored in industry and technology. The early focus in American history was upon taming the wilderness and harnessing the rivers; more recently, we have been conquering space and achieving 24-hour climate control.

On the other side of the grid, some societies believe nature dominates humans. This characteristic especially describes nomadic societies, Inuit, and some farming populations. Other societies emphasize that human beings must live in harmony with nature; nature is part of humanity and humanity is a part of nature, and human beings differ from other creatures only in degree.

Some cultures, like Western culture, tend to believe that the world and cosmos are mechanistic. Some sciences, such as chemistry and physics, assume a very mechanistic understanding of physical reality. Other cultures take a more spiritual approach; to invade nature would be blasphemous. Still others believe that human beings should exist in a kind of organic relationship with nature, not to intrude into nature nor disrupt nature.

Concerning time, some societies like ours live for the future and are driven by themes like progress and change. Americans, however, tend to focus on the near future, like bottom-line goals for next year. In some denominations, like my own, we plan only one quadrennium ahead. Some other societies have a long-term future orientation, like the Chinese, who focus hundreds of years ahead. By contrast some cultures focus mostly on the present. I am told that some American Indian tribes have no words in their language for past or future.

Of course, some conservative societies focus on the past, their valued traditions, and how to pass on their heritage. Some subgroups focus on the near past, like some American churches that are still trying to keep the 1950s alive. Other societies, like Greek culture and Arabic culture, focus on the far distant past. That is why, when you talk to some Muslims today, it is as if the Crusades occurred day before yesterday.

> Some societies stress material
> and physical goals. Other
> cultures stress spiritual goals.

In terms of the goals of life, some societies like ours stress material and physical goals. Other cultures, like Indian culture, stress spiritual goals. Still others tend to stress intellectual goals. Condon tells us no one culture puts intellectual goals at the top, but the philosophers, educators, and scholars are much more valued in some cultures than others.

Finally, some peoples believe the cosmic order is comprehensible, so we can make sense of it. Others believe the cosmos is ultimately mysterious and inscrutable. They think we cannot know about ultimate issues. Still others combine faith and reason; reason can take us so far, while faith takes us the rest of the way. On the left side of the grid, the scientific community assumes the cosmos is knowable. In the middle, the Roman Catholic Church and the theology of Thomas Aquinas would be the clearest example of the assumption that reason can take you to a certain point and faith takes you the rest of the way.

Understanding Worldviews

A people's worldview is composed of the core beliefs and values that impact behavior and provide the lens through which individuals perceive reality. How do you discover the themes of a people's worldview?

Some researchers study a people's proverbs and stories, which provide valuable clues to the culture's worldview themes. Anthropologists take a participant/observer approach and write down their observations. In the immortal words of Yogi Berra, "You can observe a lot by watching." Some researchers interview self-aware, articulate, local informants who know their culture from the inside.

I am familiar with two comprehensive grids for making sense of the worldview themes that drive a culture. One grid comes from David Burnett's book *Clash of Worlds*, which lists the following 10 guidelines for understanding a cultural group's worldview:

1. What beliefs are strongly held?
2. How do parents teach children to behave?
3. What do people regard as major offenses or sins?
4. What do people do in crises?
5. What rituals do people perform?
6. Who are the trendsetters?
7. What are people's greatest fears?
8. What are considered to be words of wisdom?
9. What art forms are expressed?
10. What aspects of the culture are most resistant to change?

Before I discovered David Burnett's list, I had worked from a number of sources to develop my own list. There is some overlap, but not much. These questions help me discover some worldview themes of a target population:

1. What are their distinctive behaviors, habits, and pastimes? What beliefs, attitudes, or values might these reflect?
2. What appear to be their goals in life? What drives them?
3. Who/what types are their heroes, heroines, and role models?
4. What are the pivotal defining events in their history?
5. What are their conscious struggles, problems, and felt needs?
6. What are their predominant beliefs and values?
7. What kinds of music do they like?
8. What are the themes of their music, stories, or legends?
9. How do they perceive the world? The past? The future?
10. What are their taboos and hang-ups? What turns them off?
11. What is their image of God? Jesus Christ? The Church? Christianity? The Bible?
12. What do they assume Christianity is basically about? Stands for? Offers? Requires in response?
13. What can we learn from those who have become Christians about approaches to effectively reach others like them?
14. What can unreached members of the target population teach us about reaching them?

To be able to answer even some of these questions helps you understand something about a people's worldview and how to share the Christian gospel with them. Other questions will occur to you as you consider questions of worldview for a particular culture.

THE WILLOW CREEK CHURCH MODEL

The Willow Creek approach to understanding a target population is another way to focus ministry on cultural needs. I believe Willow Creek Community Church is the most important apostolic experiment in 20th-century America.

When Willow Creek started in 1975, the founders interviewed many people and asked, "Do you regularly attend a local church?" If they said, "No," the next question was, "Would you

believe Willow Creek Community Church is the most important apostolic experiment in 20th-century America.

be willing to tell me why you don't?" The four answers they heard over and over again were:

1. Church is irrelevant to my issues and struggles in daily life.

2. Church and Christianity are lifeless, boring, and predictable.

3. Pastors preach down to people and they judge and condemn people.

4. Churches are always asking for money.

Bill Hybels believes every pastor should always be in conversation with at least 10 pre-Christians in their community. You can learn a lot from those folks. Then your goal from this simple field research is to write and periodically update a profile of the target population you are called to reach. You then shape your mission strategy into forms of ministry to attract the people who fit the profile. The profile called Saddleback Sam, done by Saddleback Church in southern California, is a wonderful example. Sam is described in detail in the book *The Purpose-Driven Church* (169-70). Willow Creek has a similar profile called "Unchurched Harry and Mary."

DO YOU WANT THE NEW BARBARIANS IN YOUR CHURCH?

Once you come to understand your target population, you and your church must decide whether you want these strange new people. Like the world of Ireland, Britain, and Europe from the 5th through the 10th centuries, our world is populated increasingly with the people whom I call "new barbarians." These people are not quite refined. They would not fit in most churches. They do not wear nice clothes, they do not shine their shoes, and they may have grease under their fingernails. If they did come to church, they would not know when to stand up or sit down, and in conversations they might split an infinitive or even utter an expletive!

Do we really want the new barbarians?

I was working as a consultant with a congregation in the Midwest. One afternoon, with a couple of free hours, I took my laundry to the Laundromat. While my clothes were washing and drying, I engaged eight people in conversation. Seven of the eight were not involved in any church in that community. Six of those seven had never been involved in a church in their whole life, but five of the six said they would be interested in a church if a church was interested in them. I wrote down their five names, addresses, and telephone numbers, although two of the five did not have telephones. I took the information to the leaders' group that night at church. I briefed them on the people I met at the Laundromat who said they would be interested in a church who was interested in them. One man stood up and said, "Mr. Hunter, I know the kind of people who go to that Laundromat. They are not even nice."

The more I am involved in churches, the more I become aware that most churches want to follow Jesus Christ and be fishers of men and women, but they only want to catch fish that have already been cleaned! The secular world is not giving us very many people who are just like our church members, only younger. Does your church really want these new barbarians?

WHITEHEAD'S BIG QUESTION

Alfred North Whitehead taught philosophy at Harvard and loved teaching sophomores. Once he was lecturing on cosmology and summarizing the present understanding of the universe. After class, a sophomore entered his office and said, "Professor Whitehead, you have it all wrong."

Whitehead replied, "OK, how do you understand that the universe is constituted?"

The student said, "Well, for starters, the whole thing sits on the back of a turtle."

Whitehead wondered where this eccentric fellow was coming from; he decided to buy some time. "What is that turtle standing on?"

The sophomore quickly replied, "On the back of another turtle."

Whitehead was in the process of asking what the second turtle was standing on when the sophomore interrupted: "Look, Professor Whitehead, I know what you're going to ask me, so let me just tell you—it's turtles all the way down."

Whitehead reflected on the eccentric fellow's metaphor. In his way, he had asked the ultimate question: what is it that goes all the way down?

Somehow, most of the peoples of the earth have known that if they can identify "what it is that goes all the way down," and get right with that, then their lives will be validated and justified. But God knew human beings on their own are incapable of discovering "what it is that goes all the way down." That is why it had to be revealed. We Christians are privileged to receive that revelation for the sake of others. "What it is that goes all the way down" is the creative, accepting, empowering compassion revealed in Jesus Christ. Since we have experienced reconciliation with God, justification from sin, and new life, we have no greater privilege than to share with people who have not yet experienced conversion with that reality.

The ultimate test facing the 21st-century Church will be whether we really believe the "new barbarians," who are looking for life in all the wrong places, matter to God.

If we lift up our eyes, see the harvest, and enter it in appropriate terms, Christianity in the 21st century has a magnificent future. But if we continue looking only for people who are like the people we already have, Christianity in this land does not have, nor deserve, much of a future.

▪7▪

WAKING UP YOUR DREAMS FOR REACHING THE UNCHURCHED
Dreaming God's Dreams for Your Specific Assignment

Walt Kallestad

Dreams comprised an important place in Peter's first sermon when he quoted Joel: "'In the Last Days,' God says, 'I will pour out my Spirit on every kind of people: your sons will prophesy, also your daughters; your young men will see visions, your old men dream dreams'" (Acts 2:17, TM). Reread the passage carefully. The Spirit will be poured out on every kind of people. Dreams are promised to old men and visions to young men. That's a motivating word from God to believers in all generations, including ours. Apparently God means for the old and young to dream and achieve together.

I went to Community Church of Joy in 1978 with a dream of what God wanted to help me accomplish. God gave me a dream, consistent with His promise in Acts 2, to build a mission center especially for people who had no connection with Christ or His Church. I made many discoveries as I have tried to live out His dream.

By dreams, I have in mind the distinctive hopes and vision God gives that stir our imagination and call us forward to a fantastic future. I believe it is important to discover God's dream by asking what He had in mind for us when Scripture says, "For we are God's workmanship, created in Christ Jesus to do good works, which God prepared in advance for us to do" (Eph. 2:10).

The defining discovery is for leaders to understand what God envisioned for the specific setting where He has providentially placed us.

> *To achieve anything significant, everyone needs a little imagination and a big dream."*

My own dreams are energized by Norman Vincent Peale's counsel, "To achieve anything significant, everyone needs a little imagination and a big dream." I really think God gives dreams too big for us so we have to grow into them. And in that stretching process, we find dreaming to be one of the greatest adventures in living and ministry.

As we experience this stirring of hope and vision, we need the Holy Spirit to help us sort the difference between dreaming and scheming. Scheming is what we contrive—that which we want to achieve in our own power for our own purpose. In scheming, someone else must lose so you can win. The schemer wants to know, What can I get? How does this plan benefit me? How does it make me look? While the God-directed dreamer asks, How can my accomplishment honor God? How can I significantly serve Jesus Christ? How would God be glorified and people helped if this dream was fulfilled? What does God want?

With profound, simple insight, U.S. Senate Chaplain Lloyd John Ogilvie clarifies the difference between scheming and dreaming: "Doing God's work on our own power is simply religion. But doing God's work on God's power, that's Christianity."

Dreams help us see the invisible, believe the incredible, and achieve the impossible. Great dreams require dreamers to dig beyond surface limitation, past failures, or easy-way-out distractions.

It helps me to think of the expansive components of a dream like this mathematical equation:

	Talent
plus	God's call
plus	Preparation
plus	Opportunity
equals	Waking up your dream

One small dream set in motion is powerful enough to unleash potential in other dreams and other dreamers. Then dream by dream, we can reshape the world and make our churches effective, loving, and invincible.

An acrostic built on the word *dream* helps me clarify my focus, especially as I think about creative strategies for winning secularists and for introducing the unchurched to Christ:

D   Determination
R   Risk
E   Expectation of a good outcome
A   Aspiration
M   Motivation

When those factors get mixed together, a great dream for the work of God follows almost automatically. Keep reminding yourself that risky faith, not caution, is what makes great dreams come to life. Faith makes dreams happen.

In this dreaming partnership with God, I love to remind myself and my congregation that we must allow God, the initiator of our dreams, to be the interpreter of our dreams as well as the insurer of our dreams. I've made several specific discoveries about dreaming God's dream for reaching the unchurched in my assignment as pastor at Community Church of Joy.

DREAM DISCOVERY 1—FOCUS THE DREAM

Early in our work at Phoenix, I learned how important it is to focus a dream. The dream must be sharply focused in vivid, living color. Vague dreams confuse those who want to follow your leadership and provide room for opposers to question or smother your plans. I learned that the more completely I described a dream and the more clearly I focused it, the better it would be understood and the greater likelihood it would be embraced. When people understand the dream, they are much more willing to enthusiastically connect with it and help make it come true.

I enjoy thinking about the clear-cut focus of James Nesmith's dream while he was a prisoner of war in North Vietnam for seven long years. During his imprisonment, he lived in a small, dingy cellblock with virtually no contact with anyone else. To maintain his sanity, he dreamed of playing golf. Trying to make his mental golf game as realistic as possible, he visualized every hole on his favorite course at home. He set his mind to improving his stance, his swing, and his follow-through. He played golf in his dream to the point where he could imagine where the ball landed on the course he used to play at home. He even imagined how far he would hit the ball. Some days he played 18 holes, sometimes 36 or even 72. He kept score in his mind. Before imprisonment, Nesmith was an average weekend golfer who shot in the 90s. But when Nesmith was released from prison, he returned to play his old golf course. On his first round, he shot 74. That's what a clear focus did for Nesmith.

Focused dreaming sounds like Stephen Covey's idea that we "live with the end" in mind. Here's the process. Look at what you dream of accomplishing, then start back at the beginning and describe each necessary step in living, vivid color.

I took Bill Easum on a tour of bare land where our 200-acre mission center was to be built. There were just acres and acres of dirt—nothing else. No construction had been started, no soil moved. It was difficult to get excited about this project unless you had the details clearly in your mind. I did, and I shared them with him. I described step-by-step what would unfold as this raw land was developed. I discussed the color of the buildings. I told him about the landscaping details I had in mind. I described what a day of ministry would be like at this mission center. That night when he spoke to some of our leaders, he said, "I can actually see it. I can hear the sounds of children and listen to the adults in conversation. I could even smell the gourmet coffee that was brewing."

That's exactly what I intended. I want people to see, feel, hear, and smell the dream. I was complimented to realize how my dream had been sharply focused for him. Dreams are easier to understand and easier to support when they are vividly clear.

While I do not suggest that you get carried away about making strategic plans, I think it is important to lay out your dreams and plan for their accomplishment. It was the turning point in our church when we articulated our mission statement, our vision statement, our core values, our strategic plan, and then put a business plan together. When we wrote those items down and started publicizing them, they fueled faith and energized giving. All of those planning components helped us turn the corner to launching the dream and starting to see it unfold.

I call this clear focus 20/20 dreaming. Seeing a clear, sharply focused image of your dreams is the first key to making the dream a functional reality. It is easy to waste too much of our lives and spin our wheels when we do not take time to focus our dream, to plan for it to come true, and to live it out.

DREAM DISCOVERY 2— FACE DREAM DANGERS WITH HOPE

Someone gave me a card with this clever saying, "What baking powder is to biscuits, hope is to dreams." The Bible tells us, "Let your hope make you glad" (Rom. 12:12, CEV). Most of us need to mix a lot of hope into our dreams.

When you start down the road of a great dream, conflict, criticism, and resistance to change will happen. Count on it. My experience confirms it. And you realize it is true because you have met your own dream killers.

I take courage from the Bible story about Joseph the dreamer. In Gen. 37, Joseph shared his dream with his brothers. He started by saying, "Let me tell you about my dream. We were out in the field, tying up bundles of wheat. Suddenly my bundle stood up, and your bundles gathered around and bowed down to it."

His brothers responded, "Do you really think you are going to be king and rule over us?" (vv. 6-8, CEV).

Soon Joseph had another dream, and he told his brothers, "Listen to what else I dreamed. The sun, the moon, and eleven stars bowed down to me."

When he told his father, the old man became angry and said, "What's that supposed to mean? Are your mother and I and your brothers all going to come and bow down in front of you?" (vv. 9-10, CEV).

You know the rest of the story—how his brothers grew to hate Joseph. They said to each other, "Here comes the dreamer. Let's kill him and throw him into a pit and say that some wild animal ate him. Then we will see what happens to his dreams" (cf. vv. 19-20, CEV).

The story continues with lots of misery for Joseph. He was only 17 and going across the desert alone. His family was gone and had rejected him. What pain and agony Joseph must have suffered. The rest of his experiences were not too encouraging for long years, but the dream finally came to pass.

Why would we think that when we try to carry out a God-sized dream, it will be accepted by everyone? That is not the way it works. Many of the people you serve, even some good people, will raise confusing questions and cause pain and setbacks. You may even ask God why you hurt so much when this dream is so great.

But remember Jesus warned, "If you want to follow Me, deny yourself and take up your cross." Face the dangers with hope.

As a small boy, I remember when my father, a Lutheran pastor, would come home from church council meetings, put his head in his hands, and sob. Sometimes Mom cried with him. It was terrible to watch them hurt so much. I promised myself that I would become a friend to support my pastor. I still wonder if those lay leaders in my father's churches were undermining his dream without realizing it.

But no matter, the dreamer must learn to face danger zones with hope. When going through difficult times, never forget your dream. When you face confusing change, never let the dream dim. When you cast a vision and no one seems to respond, remember the dream. When you experience conflict, remember God's promise, "I will be with you" (Isa. 43:2). When criticism comes, remember to keep your dream focused on Christ.

I remember that what God desires, He inspires. And that's where He needs dreamers like us.

DREAM DISCOVERY 3—FIND A DREAM MATE

I love the story of Connie Brown, an elementary music teacher, who needed a new dream. After years of teaching, she decided to go back to college to change her vocation but had no idea what she wanted to do. College counselors did not know how to help her because she was determined never to teach again. So they directed her to science and math. Almost by accident, she ended up in a tough physiology course without any previous understanding of the subject. She didn't even know the basic vocabulary. Her professor, who had an intimidating reputation, was incredulous when she asked Connie why she was taking the course and she answered, "For fun."

But Connie worked hard, burned the midnight oil, passed the course, earned the respect of the teacher, and was even asked to teach the professor's lab courses for several years. The professor suggested that Connie consider medical school. Aptitude tests showed her instructor's guidance should be thoughtfully considered. Today, Connie Brown is an emergency medical specialist.

Her professor became her dream mate. But what precisely does a dream mate do?

or a dreamer, a dream mate is not a luxury, but a necessity.

A dream mate is someone who sees our potential and pushes us to develop it. He or she is one who points out our strengths and helps us correct our weaknesses. A dream mate helps us say *yes* to our potential. For a dreamer, a dream mate is not a luxury, but a necessity. A dream mate helps a dreamer be realistic, honest, and committed.

Though Dr. Brown did not expect her professor to become her dream mate, she did. It is usually more helpful to intentionally seek such a person to help you dream your dreams. Some dream mates are for life, and some are involved with us only for a short time. Sometimes several different dream mates are needed for various events and phases of our lives.

Let me tell you about one who became a dream mate for me. We were trying to put together $3.2 million to buy the first 127-acre parcel of what was to become our 200-acre mission center. When I shared the dream, a little money would trickle in, but we needed millions. In frustration and hope, I called Dr. Robert Schuller and said, "I need your help. I need you to come over and talk to our people. I'll bring a bunch together, and you can ignite the dream." He agreed to come, but I didn't know what a difficult task it would be for him. He had just flown home from Africa—getting in late Saturday afternoon. He preached in all the Sunday morning services at the Crystal Cathedral, got on a private plane, and arrived in Phoenix for a Sunday afternoon meeting at three. He was so tired, he could hardly keep his eyes open; but he did exactly what I needed him to do, and I was grateful. As he walked away from the event, he paused and said, "Walt, I want you to know that I came here today because I believe in you and I believe in your dreams." With one sentence, Schuller became a dream mate who nourished and encouraged my dream. I will always be grateful for his affirmation at such a critical time in my life.

What is the profile or job description of dream mates? What do they do? And how do they help? Let me use an acrostic of *dream mate* to explain the relationship.

D   Dares to focus on significance, not simply success. Success impacts life but does not necessarily improve life. Significance impels people to move and to live far beyond where they are today. For example, when I started preaching, my wife, Mary, evaluated my sermons for significance rather than for success. The main test was that I said something relevant and transformational rather than something clever, superfluous, and successful. This idea has much to do with other phases of ministry, too, especially winning unchurched secular people. Success impacts but significance improves.

R   Responds to ideas with respect. Effective dream mates will help you explore an idea to see if it has significance. Too many ideas are discarded before they are adequately considered. The reason for dreams being prematurely discarded is that no one ever heard of such a thing before. Count on it—a dream mate never disrespects the first glimmer of an idea. Such a one helps you explore and evaluate.

E   Expects the best. Dream mates expect the best. They will not let you off with a halfhearted effort. A dream mate encourages you to try harder and to do your work better. This makes the work of ministry more effective. Too often ministry is done as if something done for God can be second-rate or third-rate. That approach is wrong because He deserves the best.

A   Affirms talents and abilities. Affirmation is like the rocket fuel for great dreams. Dream mates affirm your talents and abilities. They must be innovative in their support and genuine in their compliments. In a real sense, they become trustees of your dream.

M   Maximizes learning and growth opportunities to

improve the dream. A dream mate encourages the dreamer to continually refine the dream. A dream mate encourages a dreamer to look beyond today's challenges. Dream mates act as a kind of coach—challenging dreamers to assess where they are, to look ahead, to develop more effective strategies, and to push for greater excellence.

Think of the miraculous transformation churches would experience if every dream held by their leaders was continually being improved. Think of the new effectiveness that could be developed for helping unchurched people find Christ if every pastor in every church had a dream mate who challenged him or her to assess where he or she is, to look ahead, to develop new strategies, and to push for excellence.

M   Makes the most of mistakes and failures. It has been said that failure, when not used profitably, quickly solidifies and turns a heart to lead, making future action difficult. A dream mate makes you start again after a failure. I learned the hard way. When half of our 200 members left after my first year at Community Church of Joy, I felt like a failure, but I didn't just sit at home, stew, or complain. I committed myself to turning my failures around. God helped me kindle a more inviting, friendly environment, and the church began to grow in love as well as in numbers. Dream mates help us profit from our mistakes.

A   Accepts only excellence. Mediocrity is disastrous, especially in the church. But it happens all the time. Sadly, it is tolerated as the acceptable standard for the work of God. Most of us can do better, a lot better.

Excellence is more than doing things right; excellence is doing the right things. It is impossible for dreamers to live out their dreams by doing wrong things, even if they are done the right way. A dream mate helps keep the dreamer's conscience right and the dreamer on course to ensure excellent results. A dream mate will help us keep our commitments to excellence on track and to push for the best possible results. Great churches and productive ministries need more excellence.

T   Takes time to give honest feedback. Time and feedback are key functions of dream mates. A dreamer needs dream mates who take time to evaluate and nourish the relationship. When dreamers do not get honest feedback, they are likely to derail or digress. Honest feedback requires fearless evaluation of what attitudes and actions are moving the dreamer closer or farther from accomplishing the dream. Often dreamers are too close to the situation to realize what factors are slowing their progress. This feedback is not achieved by condemnation or criticism, but by helping the dreamer maximize his or her abilities and opportunities, thus moving the dreamer more effectively toward realizing the dream.

E   Encourages perseverance. Dr. Robert Schuller tells about a trip to Africa where he was overcome with emotion by the hardships the people suffered. He found he could not speak and had tears in his eyes as he stood to address the people. Almost immediately a man stood up and walked toward Dr. Schuller and said, "Among our people, we will not let anyone cry alone." That level of support helps the dreamer keep trying until he or she succeeds.

Every dreamer needs someone who will be loyal through thick and thin. Every dreamer needs a dream mate to encourage him or her to live life to the fullest. Too many Christian leaders quit or move on when the going gets tough. I guess they are looking for comfort more than character development or achievement for Jesus. Many have started with dreams, but they gave up too quickly, either because of fear or lack of resources. But I encourage you to hang in there, follow through, and persevere. If it is God's dream, it is well worth giving your life for it.

Every dreamer needs a dream mate who will help him or her take the long view and keep a clear perspective. Winston Churchill is famous for his words, "Never give up. Never give up. Never give up." That's what we need. The effective dream mate says, "Go for it. You can do it. I believe in you. It's possible. Keep going."

DREAM DISCOVERY 4—TAKE CHRIST INTO YOUR DREAMS

In 1989, as I was working on my doctorate at Fuller Seminary, I was in a hotel room and needed to find out if God planned for me to continue at Community Church of Joy. We had completed a 10-year strategic plan. We had exceeded what the plan called us to do, and it was time to evaluate my work and life. I needed to understand the next chapter.

I took time for prayer and fasting one afternoon. I prayed, "God, what do You want?" I got down on my knees about 3 P.M., and before I realized it, it was dark outside, and it was about 11 P.M. That was the time that the dream of developing our mission center with something for every age began to develop in my heart. I started writing the details down. And it stretched my comfort zone.

I'll never forget when I returned home and met the church board. They tease me now that they don't want me to go away anymore because of the big dreams God gave me that day in the hotel.

When I arrived back in Phoenix on Friday, I decided to get the group together on Sunday night. I was scared. I was shaking inside as I told them I had something on my heart that I needed to share with them. I was frightened of their rejection, because the plan seemed absolutely impossible. After I finished my presentation, we spent time praying. Soon our prayers were, "Well, God, if this is what You want, You are going to have to help us find land." We agreed we would take steps in faith to find out if this was what He wanted.

Someone soon found a piece of land that we thought had potential. We stood on the land. It was mud. We stood ankle deep in the mud and prayed, "If You want us in this place, make it happen." That is the land we finally secured to fulfill the dream.

You see, the dream was in God's mind before it was in our mind. When we went looking for the owner of the property, I came in contact with Scottie, who was 87, and his wife, Ruthie. Though he didn't own the land, he had lived on it for many years. As I knocked on the door, I said, "I'm Rev. Kallestad. I am a pastor, and we believe God is calling us to buy this orange grove and build a mission center here. We want to build a church."

Scottie invited me in. I sat by a table that had pictures of Christ and Billy Graham above it. So I knew I was in friendly territory. I told Scottie and Ruthie about our dreams. Then they told me about their dream: 40 years ago they started walking around this very piece of land, praying God would one day build a great church there.

Here's the incredible part—I was 9 years old when they

started to pray. I was a little boy when God planted seeds of our dream in the hearts of Scottie and Ruthie. That was strong confirmation for me and our church board that the dream was God's dream.

Whether or not you find a loyal, wise, compassionate, human dream mate, I encourage you to turn to one dream mate who has proven to be reliable and trustworthy beyond my wildest imagination. My most trusted dream mate is Jesus Christ, who goes before me to show the way, walks beside me to befriend me, stands behind me to encourage me, hovers over me to watch after me, and lives within me to fill me with peace. He will go the distance with you.

This prayer, attributed to St. Patrick, gives a call that challenges each of us to listen for God as He speaks to us about our dreams—directly to our spirit, through His Word, or through a friend or stranger. You always have a dream mate when you include God in your dreams.

> *Christ be with me, Christ within me,*
> *Christ behind me, Christ before me,*
> *Christ beside me, Christ to win me,*
> *Christ to comfort and restore me,*
> *Christ beneath me, Christ above me,*
> *Christ in quiet, Christ in danger,*
> *Christ in mouth of friend or stranger.*

DREAM DISCOVERY 5—WATCH FOR GOD'S APPROVAL

In fulfilling our dreams for God and building great churches, we need to rejoice in God's commitments to us. It is not only that we believe in God, but that God believes in us. It is not only how much we love God, but how much God loves us. In developing the mission center, there have been days of great discouragement and continual challenge. But God called us to fulfill the dream, and He keeps affirming it. It is His commitment to us, and we rejoice in it.

At one point our church was at a crossroads where we needed to come up with $2 million. We did not have it, and we did not know where to get it. So we asked the Father, "How are we going to meet this need?"

One afternoon soon after that prayer, I was in my office

when the phone rang. The caller was a banker who wanted to speak with me. He said, "Pastor, you know there is a lady that we told you about a few years ago who was considering remembering your church in her will." I think she was about 98 when we first heard about it, and no one expected her to follow through. The banker continued, "She died at 102 years of age and left your church $2 million." This lady had never been to our church. She was raised Catholic, and I never met her. I had nothing to do with her remembering us in her will. Neither did anyone in our church. That's a sign of God's approval of our dream.

Another amazing thing about the fulfillment of this mission center dream is to discover what is happening in the hearts of our people as the dream unfolds. To me, it is not so impressive that we will have buildings, roads, and facilities. But it is a joy to watch what happens in the hearts of our people as we live out this dream together. Their faith is growing to the point of becoming gigantic. Think how much that stretches their souls and gets them ready for more adventures with God in the future.

The dream also impacts outsiders. I think of Tony, who was in his 70s and had never darkened a church door. In fact, when I went to see Tony for the first time, he got so nervous he had diarrhea. I don't think we realize how frightened people are of Christians, especially ministers. He was the owner of the land we needed. I told Tony he needed to come to church to really experience what God had waiting for him, that he was missing out.

"Ah," he said, "I don't think I am interested."

I said, "Well, will you come for just a moment?" So the next Sunday he came and stood in the back. He opened the door cautiously. I saw this tall, imposing figure stand there for less than a minute. Then he disappeared.

The next week I called him and said, "Tony, you need to come again and bring your wife. You need to come in and sit down and experience worship with us."

He came the following Sunday with his wife and sat near the back door so he could escape if necessary. It was a dangerous, risky endeavor for him. He came the next week, and then I called him. He said, "You know, Walt, that was really good. Never experienced anything like that before."

In a few weeks, he came down front after worship and said, with tears in his eyes, "Walt, do you have to be born again to be a Christian?"

I replied, "Well, yes, you do; but I would like to talk to you about what that means." So the next week we got together for lunch, and Tony welcomed Christ into his life.

"I know that God must be really angry at me," Tony said. "I don't know if He'll forgive me. I've done some really bad things in my life."

Tony was changed. His office staff knew it. And his wife said, "I am married to a different man. Everything has changed in Tony's life."

Shortly after that, I got a call in the middle of the night from the hospital. Tony had an aneurysm and died. And at his funeral, I felt such indescribable joy as I realized Tony died as a Christian. That is what our dreams are all about—being partners with Christ in changing lives.

The Lord's approval gives me confidence because I know He will give me what I need rather than what I want. My dream wants are generated from my limited human understanding. Settling for what I want will never ultimately satisfy me or make the best use of my potential for God. Knowing Christ wants what is best for my present and my future, I trust His guidance and seek His approval. He has all the wisdom and knowledge I need. He has the incredible power to do more than I could ever do. His approval energizes and empowers our achievements.

Dream Discovery 6—Dreamers Need Renewal

In working to focus the church on meeting needs of contemporary people, the dreamer may sometimes experience weariness, frustration, fatigue, and loneliness. The hard work and annoying aggravations may temporarily dim the dream. If dreamers do not constantly monitor and renew their dreams, they sometimes suffer a blackout of power. How can needed renewal be accomplished?

If your dreams are flickering, it's time to check your power connections. Character grounded in God's standards of integrity, responsibility, generosity, perseverance, and forgiveness has power to protect our dreams from shorting out or blowing up. Even though no one has perfect performance in ministry, character always counts much more than credentials. Our basic character affects our dreams, including our motivations, our methods, and our results.

Our character is resourced by God. When an electrical appliance fails to work, we check to see if we have a faulty connection to the power source. Dreamers need to ensure they are connected to the divine source. The Bible is our connection to God, who is the one true source of power. In the Bible, Paul advised the Philippians to act on a strategy for positive, power-filled thinking: "Whatever is true, whatever is noble, whatever is right, whatever is pure, whatever is lovely, whatever is admirable—if anything is excellent or praiseworthy—think about such things" (4:8).

Remind yourself daily to choose to believe what is true, noble, right, and praiseworthy about yourself, your dreams, and other people—particularly anyone criticizing you. This prevents short circuits of self-pity and bitterness. It may even be helpful if you imagine yourself trashing the untrue, ignoble, wrong, impure, ugly, and disrespectful attitudes. And then wrap yourself in wisdom and understanding. Repeated practice in focusing on the pure and true makes it easier to get rid of the negatives before they blow a fuse and cut the power to your dream.

DREAM DISCOVERY 7—DREAMS MUST BE AWAKENED

Dreams must be encouraged and awakened. Great dreaming is not putting your head in the clouds. That merely obscures your view of the world and produces no positive results. Great dreaming, rather, is like cloud seeding. Meteorologists study the clouds and actively seek ways to bring positive good out of the clouds—rain—down to the earth. Cloud seeding involves planting clouds with tiny solid particles—things like dry ice or silver iodide—that encourage raindrop formation and bring the life-giving potential of the clouds to the earth to foster growth and renew life.

Vision, imagination, creativity, and action are particles that great dreamers can build into their dreams. Around these, the life-giving potential of effective solutions, innovation, and positive change can form, fostering growth and renewing life.

Keeping dreams alive and alert to the possibilities may sometimes even mean examining things upside down and inside out, turning the kaleidoscope in the light of God's truth rather than holding it fixed in what passes as conventional wisdom.

Open your eyes to all the possibilities around you. One day Helen Keller struck up a conversation with a friend who had just returned from a long walk in the woods. When Helen asked her what she had observed, the friend answered, "Nothing, really." Helen wondered how anyone could walk in the woods for an hour and not notice anything special. She thought how she, though blind and deaf, could feel the texture of the trees, smell the fragrance of the flowers, and imagine the forest around her; she marveled that her friend, though gifted with sight and hearing and other senses, could not see as much. Keller's life is an inspiration and challenge to everyone to fully perceive the possibilities life offers all of us.

God's intention for you—for everyone—is that you not miss even the smallest possibilities that could be the seed for a raindrop to bring renewal and growth to your life and to your ministry. Be alert to the possibilities of God-inspired dreams all around you.

Consider what radical dreaming could mean for the church you serve. Dream about what God wants your church to be. Dream about how God wants to increase your influence for Him. Dream about how the gospel can be effectively communicated to secularists in your setting. Dream about what God wants to do through your church as a redemptive force in your community. Dream about what is the holiest, happiest, most influential accomplishment God wants to do through you in your present assignment.

God's promise is that you will "dream dreams" and "see visions" and that "everyone who calls on the name of the LORD will be saved. . . . The promise is for you and your children and for all who are far off—for all whom the Lord our God will call" (Acts 2:17, 21, 39).

▪ 8 ▪

MAKING CHILDREN AND YOUTH A HIGHER PRIORITY

Christ's Mandate— "Bring the Children to Me"*

Tom Benjamin

Children acting like children at church make us rejoice at Light of the World Christian Church in downtown Indianapolis. Both their laughter and unpredictable behavior assure us we are obeying our Lord's directive, "Bring the children to me."

I know it is a little unsettling to some to hear babies cry or children act like children, but in our congregation, we strongly believe that giving high priority to children and teens pleases the Lord. It attracts many adults, increases attendance, and expands our influence into the community.

As might be expected, parents feel embarrassed when a child talks too loudly or sings at the wrong time. Crying infants and noisy preteens sometimes distract others from worship. From experience, we know how a fussy preschooler can interrupt a service. Such distractions may hinder concentration on my sermon, maybe even spoil my own concentration.

But such interruptions also help us know our church is alive and has a future. They assure us we are not dead or dying. At the same time, these distractions subtly remind everyone that children are welcome at Light of the World Christian Church. Our congregation values children for who they are as well as what they can become. For us, children are the church of today as much as they are the church of tomorrow.

*Author's paraphrase of Mark 10:14. Used other places in this chapter.

Biblical Directive

What we learned at Light of the World—putting children first—is thoroughly biblical and amazingly simple. We also believe it is right. What a combination—it is biblical, simple, and right. Adults need children and generally go where children are. But when a church focuses exclusively on an adult agenda, they seldom attract children. On the contrary, a church usually serves more adults when children are given high priority. Children attract adults. Watch how adults love to be with children in malls, restaurants, and on the streets.

At our church we take Jesus' instruction seriously: "You must become as a child if you want to enter the kingdom" (Mark 10:15, author's paraphrase). But if a church has no children, it is difficult to become like one. We all need children in our lives. They are fair, fun, and flexible. And Jesus wants us to become more and more like them.

New Paradigm

Prioritizing children and youth in a church's ministry was a new paradigm for me—a brand-new way of thinking about the work of the church. I did it the old way for 30 years. We had children's Sunday School, sometimes had children's Christmas or Easter pageants, and provided an out-of-date, crowded nursery. Perhaps once a year we had Children's Sunday, sometimes on Children's Day.

And when we had enough teens to have a youth group, we offered parties and athletics. Meanwhile, we hoped and prayed they would not create a ruckus to worry parents and old folks. Once a year, we had Youth Sunday with a speaker whom the adults would like. I love to joke that we generally invited speakers who were in charge of the youth section of AARP—not too old, but a long ways from young.

> *Children and youth are at frightening risk in our society.*

Present Tragedy

Since the old paradigm hasn't worked, it's time for the church to stop sleeping through the current youth revolution.

Children and youth are at frightening risk in our society. Nearly everyone knows the problems. But let me ask, Can't your church hear our children crying from the schools, the streets, and the gangs? Can't we recognize fear among latchkey kids and babies having babies? Can't we see the alarming loss of innocence as they watch sex and violence on TV?

How many more children must be killed in school shootings before we do something to stop it?

How many more teen pregnancies will we witness before we mobilize righteous forces to change the problem?

How many more gang murders will we read about before we seek the face of God?

How many more children must be abused before we say, "Stop it"?

How many more secular people do we have to raise before we invest our God-given resources to win them while they are young?

How long before we repent for not invading the world of children with our Savior's message?

How long? How long? How long?

Action Needed

Let's face today's realities in church and community. While we church people talk and talk and talk, and sometimes wring our hands, a new generation grows into adulthood without possessing what God expects us to give them. It's easy to blame society, working parents, schools, divorce, television, secularism, and hundreds of other influences.

Still the church must take some blame for its deafening, too-little-too-late response to children's needs. But no amount of blame saves kids. No amount of blame will correct the mistakes we have made with earlier generations. It is a fact; we have had enough talk. Action is now needed in every home, school, and church. And since the home and school appear to be even weaker than the church, let's say our prayers, roll up our sleeves, and get started.

Robert Coles, prize-winning author and psychiatry professor at Harvard Medical School, in his book *The Moral Intelligence of Children,* has amazing encouragement for us: "Our sons and daughters, our students, of whatever age, are on the lookout for moral direction" (169). Since it is obvious children do not get such directions at home or school—quite the contrary—the church must take radical and risky action.

One child development expert spoke of abuses in daycare centers: "We are cannibalizing children. Children are dying in this system, never mind achieving optimum development." What he says about day care may be even more true in the culture as a whole. In many settings, this is not a good time to be a kid.

Therefore, our churches must take significantly more responsibility to fill this moral void that is leading our children into cesspools of moral decay. As go our children, so goes the church and so goes the society.

Ministry to children and teens must be massively increased both because of the need and because of the positive differences it will bring to our churches and society. One of the most overlooked principles of church health and church growth is giving children a higher priority rather than merely giving them a program.

Such a commitment should not be made to increase numbers or income, though that might result. Rather, we must accept the challenge because it must be done. And like every other ministry in the church, when we do what is right and do what is needed, money comes from somewhere, and personnel will be drawn to such a worthy cause. One of the main characteristics of a healthy church is the way it treats children.

Next-Door Mission Field

Much as we would willingly and generously respond to a ripe-for-harvest overseas mission field, I challenge every church to expand and improve its ministry to children and youth. Notice I said ministry, not program. Make an honest attempt to find out how many needy, unchurched children reside in your community—you'll be shocked by the number. After you know for sure, ask the Father what your responsibility is to the little ones.

Why do it? Our reasons are reasons of the heart. Josh, Sarah, and Ashley need the positive influence of the gospel. It will affect their lives and the lives of their children's children. It will enable parents to know how to develop their children's moral and spiritual capacities, something they often do not know how to do or, in some cases, have lost the moral authority to do. Society will be benefited as the gospel reforms destructive

> *he Lord will be pleased by your efforts to love children the way He did.*

behaviors and exposes secular values for what they are. The Lord will be pleased by your efforts to love children the way He did. The church will grow in influence and numbers—it means dealing with numbers that really count. As a by-product, adults who have children and those without children will be impressed and attend because of the attention you place on children.

Everyone involved in helping in this great effort will experience the incredible satisfaction of being part of a great cause whose impact is eternal. Our motivation for giving children and youth priority in the church is a reason of the heart.

LET ME SHARE MY MINISTRY METAMORPHOSIS

Early in my life, I identified with children who are hurting because I came from a broken home. From age five, I was raised by a single-parent grandmother, and I owe her so much. Though a spirit of wonder filled my childhood, I still felt pain from not having a family life with two loving parents. My sainted grandmother made it her business never to let me come home to an empty house or an empty heart. It is my own sense of loss plus the wonderful influence of my grandmother that make me passionate about the plight of children. The predicament makes me cry, even today.

The current crisis among children shapes my ministry and values. I can hear children crying from a thousand sources in our society. I feel committed to make a difference through the church and work like a passionate evangelist to get other pastors to take up the cause.

After I graduated from St. Louis University, my first job was with the Division of Child Welfare in Cleveland. I worked as a caseworker, protecting and resourcing children who lived in foster homes.

During the first years in that assignment, the Lord called me into the ministry. While I was in seminary, I served as a youth minister. I took that assignment because I was available and the right age, not because I was able or gifted. I learned early in that job that most churches are adult organizations that do not want their adult agenda challenged.

When I finished seminary at age 26, I preached my first sermon as a senior pastor. The sermon was titled "Under New Management." Reality soon set in as I developed my pastoring skills and priorities. During those first 15 years, nearly everything changed in the church—I thought of myself as a change agent, and the congregation agreed. The church grew dramatically, as did our influence, yet I knew something was missing.

What Is Missing?

After 14 years of ministry, I began to feel a yearning to fill an emptiness in the church. By God's grace, I had taken a sleepy, mainline church in a lackadaisical Midwestern city—Indianapolis—from a few hundred to several thousand members. The church moved from obscurity to a degree of national prominence. Yet I felt as if I was pulling an 18-wheeler up Mount Everest with the gearbox locked in reverse.

After those years as pastor at Light of the World Christian Church, we had a new church building and a growing congregation, but we still had many old demons. As I cried out to God in prayer, I reminded Him, "My church isn't what I want it to be. My people are not responsive. My congregation is doing little that really matters. Is this all there is?"

God replied about that time, "First, little brother, it's not your church. It's My church. You do the teaching and preaching, do your best to motivate and inspire, and I will do the rest." So I did what He said, and God did what He promised.

Can You Hear the Crying?

A large part of what God showed me were the needs, cries, and suffering of children in every sector of American culture. Being an African-American pastor, I felt a crushing burden for children in Black communities.

God began to break my heart with problems facing Black children. The focus God gave me centered mostly on Black boys on their way to manhood. The issues became clear: How does the little boy become a real man who heads a family and takes a place of meaningful involvement in church and community? Given our present problems in our inner cities, how will these boys who are moving so quickly toward biological adulthood find their way to spiritual and emotional manhood? How can they make it when so many little boys have to go it alone with so few male role models to follow?

All this time, I never thought to evaluate my paradigm for youth ministry. So we followed old, established, ineffective ways of serving children and youth. Soon the Lord clearly directed me to understand that children and teens were to have a much higher priority in my ministry and in the work of our church.

The tears began to flow. I had to do much more through the church. I thought about my own sons. I thought about our ministry to children. From those holy nudges in my inner person, I was inspired to write this poem detailing the difference between what God wants and what the culture gives our children:

I hurt for boys whose maturity gets mugged by materialism.
I hurt for boys who are raped by racism.
I hurt for boys who allow themselves to become gutted by greed.
I hurt for boys who contact AIDS before they come of age.
I hurt for boys who get into crack before they get into church.
I hurt for boys who get into gangs before they get into God.
I hurt for boys who get into hip-hop before they get into holiness.
I hurt for boys who get into pistols before they get into prayers.
I hurt for boys who get into jail before they get into Jesus.

Starting a Revolution for God

Lest anyone think I am slighting girls and young women, let me clearly express that I believe they face similar problems that are only intensified because Black males often grow up to be irresponsible husbands and absent fathers. I am fully committed to give attention to all our children and give the gospel an opportunity to transform their lives early and thoroughly.

And lest anyone think I am leaving out children of other colors and other cultures, I want to go on record that children everywhere are spiritually at risk. That means every church has to move rapidly to do everything it can to save all the children.

> *very church has to move rapidly to do everything it can to save all the children.*

In my ministry metamorphosis, as I worked out the details of this new dream, I preached a message on TV on the topic of how males in our communities can be helped to move from boys to men. When that message was first aired on TV, the response was phenomenal. It seems we are onto something important for God. I have enjoyed confirmation for the ideas in many ways from community, church, culture, and Christ.

OUR MANDATE FROM OUR MASTER

The message is abundantly clear: Jesus wants children cherished in the church. He wants children and childlike adults in His ministry. Put your ear down to Mark 10:13-16, and listen carefully.

His directive is definite; there can be no doubt what He expects. Contrary to His usual affirming reaction to the disciples, His tone in this passage is tough, even annoyed. At the same time, His attitude toward children and their parents is tender and loving. And His expectations for us to be childlike in Kingdom relationships is as clear as the morning sun. The Bible really teaches us much about these issues in only four verses.

I have been reading the passage recently in Eugene H. Peterson's paraphrase *The Message*. His use of contemporary language makes the meaning even more apparent:

"The people brought children to Jesus, hoping he might touch them. The disciples shooed them off. But Jesus was irate and let them know it: 'Don't push these children away. Don't ever get between them and me. These children are at the very center of life in the kingdom. Mark this: Unless you accept God's kingdom in the simplicity of a child, you'll never get in.' Then, gathering the children up in his arms, he laid his hands of blessing on them."

Transform Mandate to Mission

At Light of the World Christian Church, we direct our ministry by our well-crafted and thoroughly prayed-over mission statement: "Jesus is our message, people are our mission, and soul winning is our business." We understand one of the most significant ways we can accomplish our mission is in the rescue, preparation, and empowerment of children. And after long consideration of the Mark passage and after much concern for the needs of children in our society, our church has concluded that our ministry to children and youth must be more than auxiliary or adjunct to other ministries.

So much of what many contemporary churches do has little to do with the gospel and even less with what Jesus actually did.

We are coming to believe more and more that our work is not only to preach about Jesus but also to do what Jesus did. We want to follow our Master by loving children, by touching them, and by welcoming them into His kingdom. So much of what many contemporary churches do has little to do with the gospel and even less with what Jesus actually did. Yet the Bible pattern is to preach His gospel and follow His example.

Now concerning children, we can no longer "shoo . . . them off" as the disciples did—because that irritates our Lord. And we dare not hinder children in any way because He said, "Don't ever get between them and me."

The mandate is crystal clear: welcome children, understand their significance to the Kingdom, and become childlike if you are serious about being part of Christ's kingdom. That's our Christ-directed mandate.

SPECIFIC STRATEGIES FOR IMPLEMENTING THE MANDATE

Now after the mandate is clearly understood, a leader has to ask how we make children a priority in the ministry we do for the Lord Jesus in our churches. Let me propose several suggestions.

1. Get a clear perspective. Understanding conditions children face helps us know what children need. That is true at every level of society, whether we work in rural settings, suburbs, or urban environments.

Our perspective also has to be shaped by the kind of church we want to have and the kind of country we want to live in. Hillary Clinton's sentence is right: "How well we care for our own and other people's children isn't only a question of morality; our self-interest is at stake too."

The perspective must also take into account that children are a tremendous resource. They are a wonderful part of the church today and will carry what we invest in them into the tomorrows. We shape their personal future by our ministry to them today, and they in turn set the destiny of the church for the future.

The other perspective that is needed is to accurately assess what our particular church is doing for children. Check your attitudes and activities against Mark 10. How does your church measure up? How do you measure up to what God wants?

2. Develop a passion for children. Give careful consideration to their potential and plight. In developing your passion, consider this challenge: "Whatever makes you cry is something you have been assigned to heal." Most of us follow the tracks of our tears.

We really do not have an adolescent problem, but an adult problem fueled by lack of vision, disobedience to the Word, and self-indulgence."

I love this quote because it clarifies the issues so well for me: "We really do not have an adolescent problem, but an adult problem fueled by lack of vision, disobedience to the Word, and self-indulgence." Sometimes I don't want to hear that because it judges me.

Writers on renewing pastoral passion are saying it over and over in conferences and books—our passion must be based on what Jesus was passionate about. After a careful, personal study of Mark 10, I am convinced ministry to children certainly qualifies as something Jesus felt passionate about.

The contemporary church suffers from lack of passion—passion for lost souls, for hurting people, and specifically for children. But when we increase our passion for what really matters to Jesus, it seems to me that all of heaven opens to us. Resources, satisfaction, and effectiveness follow.

3. Understand your present position is based on the attitude of leaders. Our attitude toward children determines the kind of ministry we provide for them. In too many places, we have a serious problem with contemporary lay and clergy disciples who say or think, "Don't bring the children into the regular service." But if children are never in services with adults, will they ever feel as if they belong or even own the church?

To check your attitudes, seek the mind of Christ concerning the details of your ministry to children in your present assignment. If children do not have a high priority, you may be out of harmony with what Jesus wants for your church.

What we believe about lost people and what we think about God must be built into our thinking about children. In most churches, adults get top billing because they give the money and build the budget. But thousands of dying, boring churches could have a new lease on life and a new approval from the Lord if they would change their individual and corporate attitudes toward serving children. And when we begin to see that all children are as important to God as our own biological children, it is easier to change the priorities and easier to raise necessary funds.

4. Give children high visibility. If you believe what the Bible says and practice what you believe, the need for higher visibility is clear.

Another important factor that fuels our motivation to serve children is to remember how many of us as children were loved into Christ's kingdom by some adult. We shouldn't get far from that fact because it makes us want to pass the benefit on.

The changes we have made in favor of children at our church are nearly revolutionary. Every Sunday, several young people work with me at the pulpit and on the platform. Every

Sunday, junior deacons help with details of the service. Every Sunday, youth ushers help people find seats and gather the offering. Young musicians play every Sunday. Every third Sunday, an

E very Sunday, several young people work with me at the pulpit and on the platform.

officer of the church takes Communion to shut-ins, and the young people go along to help serve and offer comfort in the name of Jesus. Kids are everywhere in our church, and we love it. So do they.

At least once a month, I bless the children in the name of Jesus. I call them down front and tell them, "I want to bless you." Each time I call for a different age-group, so everyone in that age-group comes forward at the same time. I boldly proclaim, "I take authority over the enemy that wants to destroy you and assure you that our Lord is bigger than all the problems the devil can dream up for you. I bless you in the name of Jesus." Our Lord blessed children and touched them, and so do I. Mark 10:16 says of Jesus, "He . . . put his hands on them and blessed them." Such a touch from a pastor on a regular basis has unbelievable influence on kids when they face peer pressure or temptation; it is a wonderful prevention that keeps them from making many harmful choices.

Many youth ministries get prime-time exposure, even Sunday morning. The children will not always give a perfect performance, but neither do the adults. Don't be afraid to take a chance on putting children up front. God takes a chance on us every Sunday.

Interestingly enough, in place of the deadly monotony we often experienced before, we now have interest and optimism. Shared time on Sunday morning has created an intergenerational integration between ministries, which we love at our church.

Many churches are dead and dying. Or they are old, stale, and boring in the ways they do ministry. To avoid these problems, the church has to be true to Christ and relevant to our times. What's more relevant now than kids?

5. Take advantage of the growth potential of children and youth. Look realistically at yourself in the mirror. You will see you are on your way to being history, but children are the church's bridge to the future. They represent potential, destiny, and possibility. Children will help your church grow a thousand times faster than all the gimmicks you can dream up.

As a marvelous serendipity of giving high visibility and priority to children, you will experience growth in numbers, interest, and finance from adults who believe in what you are doing. Adults want to be where their children, grandchildren, and neighborhood children are. For the few who gripe that children are not important, you will find many more who rejoice that you are following the Lord Jesus in your ministry. Remember, it is our Lord who commands and commissions us to "bring the children to me."

THE REWARDS FOR SERVING CHILDREN

The payback for serving children is inspirationally explained in Dr. David McKenna's commentary on Mark 10 in *The Communicator's Commentary*. McKenna is president emeritus of Asbury Seminary, writer, preacher, and Christian statesman. In his commentary on this passage, he points out that the words "He [Jesus] took the children in His arms" can be amplified to mean, "He folded them into His arms."

What a picture that is for the contemporary church and for hurting children around us. We can fold children into the arms of faith and hope.

McKenna helps me even more with his reminder that children who experience love will return the love. To put his idea into a human picture, he tells about a visit to a refugee camp in Cambodia.

Here's the story in his words:

We came to a clearing where our guide suggested we take a picture with our college students who were serving food to the refugees. Lining up for a typical camera shot, we noticed two Cambodian children had followed us into the circle. I stopped the picture and beckoned to a little brown boy, asking that he come and pose with me. At first he hesitated, then, looking at his sister for approval, he took half-

steps toward me. I went over and scooped him up. Bare
bones protruded through the flesh into my hands as I felt
starvation for the first time. Emotions that I had known only at the dedication of my own children engulfed me as I
folded that boy into my arms. Then, just before the shutter
clicked, he snuggled his head into the crook of my neck in a
show of love that I will feel through eternity. At that moment, our love was perfect and our trust complete. I would
have walked a continent with him in my arms in order to
claim him as my son, or I would have taken his place in a
Cambodian hut if I could have assured his future. Neither
of these choices was mine to make, but the meaning of the
moment can never be taken away from me. . . . For the
present, I am content to know that I have had the privilege
of entering into the Spirit of Jesus Christ when He folded
the children into His arms and they snuggled their heads into the crook of His neck (*Mark,* in *The Communicator's Commentary,* 207).

That's what Jesus meant when He instructed us, "Bring the
children to me." That is what He wanted us to understand when
He said, "Anyone who will not receive the kingdom of God like
a little child will never enter it." And that is the joy He wants us
to feel when we do as He did when He "put his hands on them
and blessed them" (Mark 10:15-16).

Putting children in high priority in your ministry will expand your soul, save a child, win families, change the world, and
grow your church.

"Bring the children to me." What a challenge. What an opportunity.

■ 9 ■

"DOING CHURCH" TO REACH PRE-CHRISTIAN PEOPLE

Viable Ministry to the American Mission Field

George Hunter III

I have traveled my own denomination and others enough to know that, in the U.S.A., there are tens of thousands of Mickey Mouse churches—spinning their ecclesiastic wheels, beehives of activity, absorbed in good church work without ever getting around to doing the real work of the Church. They have never faced the fact that, in the words of William Temple, "the church is the only society on earth raised up for the sake of its nonmembers." These churches assume that activity is achievement and that maintaining the status quo fulfills their reason for being.

Meanwhile, our churches exist in an increasingly secular environment in which growing numbers of people have never been substantially influenced by the Christian religion. These people don't know what we are talking about; they have no Christian memory. Many postmodern people are no longer buying the rationalistic ideology of the Enlightenment. More right-brained than left-brained, they are looking more for experience than for reasons. They are receptive—searching for something and willing to try anything, from astrology to Zen, from sex to steroids. They turn to all kinds of things in an effort to find something upon which to norm, inform, and complete their lives.

Of the 120 million or more functionally secular in the U.S.A., most have almost nothing to do with the church. Some of them surveyed have a church preference—Presbyterian, Methodist, Lutheran, or whatever—which merely identifies the church they stay away from. They do come, still in fair numbers, for baptisms, weddings, and funerals. As one English wag puts it, they come to be "hatched, matched, and dispatched." Then you don't see them again for months, years, or decades.

FRIGHTENING CONCLUSIONS
ABOUT TRADITIONAL CHURCHES

In the midst of this fast-growing mission field, most traditional churches do not reach secular people. The mind-set says if they want to come, they are welcome. But why should we change to reach them? I venture five conclusions about traditional churches and their lack of effect on contemporary society.

1. Most Christians in traditional churches virtually never share their faith and invite others. One study indicates that it takes the average Episcopalian 28 years to make another Episcopalian convert.

2. Most traditional churches cannot reach and retain pre-Christian secular people. It almost never happens. Indeed, the core leaders may be so involved in the church that they may not know many pre-Christian people. They assume that because they don't know many, there aren't many!

3. Most traditional churches have no plans to reach secular pre-Christian people. They never pray for it to happen. If God suddenly gave the average traditional church 50 active new seekers, they would not know what to do with them.

4. Most traditional churches today cannot retain even a bare majority of their own young people into adult discipleship. The secular society has much more influence on our young people than the church.

5. The culture around our churches has changed enormously since the 1950s. Today, most traditional churches so badly misfit the surrounding culture that it is impossible to graft a good evangelism program onto a traditional church and expect anything to happen for more than a season.

Indeed, many traditional churches seem to expect next year to be 1957! That means we have churches strategically positioned all over this land so that if 1957 ever comes around again, they will be effective. But if history does *not* do a U-turn, traditional churches are on a trajectory to become the Amish of the 21st century. The churches who blindly perpetuate the forms of

M*any traditional churches seem to expect next year to be 1957!*

an early era into a drastically changed culture are doomed to failure. Samuel Shoemaker's haunting question, asked a half century ago, has never been more imperative: "Can your kind of church reach this kind of world?" Indeed, can we even engage people in this kind of changed world? If not, why not reconsider the way you do church?

THE ABIDING PREREQUISITES FOR DOING CHURCH

Naturally, the faithful church in any generation must have a changeless foundation—the gospel. The gospel does not change, but the forms through which we communicate its meaning should change as the culture changes. Furthermore, there are several other blocks that are necessary to the foundation.

I am especially posing this question: What kind of church develops and empowers its people for outreach to secular, postmodern people? I am aware of at least five foundation blocks that a church has to have in place to some substantial degree if the church is to reach pre-Christian people. The blocks do not guarantee effectiveness, but the church cannot be a *Christian* church without them:

1. Does the church deeply believe Christianity is a revealed religion? Lyle Schaller, in *Tattered Trust,* says there is an increasingly great divide in churches today between those who believe Christianity is a revealed religion and those who believe Christianity is merely an imagined religion. I am suggesting that faithful churches in the apostolic tradition deeply believe that Christianity is a revealed religion that has been entrusted with the gospel for everybody. A congregation may not even *deserve* to have a viable future as a Christian church if it does not substantially meet that prerequisite.

2. Does the church root its people and its ministry in Scripture? No church can be a faithful apostolic church without placing the Bible at the center of its life.

he faithful, effective church has a wholehearted sense of dependence on God.

3. Is the church disciplined and expectant in prayer? The faithful, effective church has a wholehearted sense of dependence on God.

4. Does the church like lost people? Does the church understand lost people? Does the church have compassion for lost, pre-Christian people? I have interviewed many secular folks who have visited churches who reported not being understood, liked, loved, or even wanted.

5. Is obedience to the Great Commission the church's main business? Or is outreach merely one of many (more or less equal) purposes that the church is driven by? If mission does not function as something like a magnificent obsession, the church will not gather much harvest.

WHAT KIND OF CHURCH EMPOWERS ITS PEOPLE FOR OUTREACH?

Now to the question, What kind of church empowers its people for outreach, attracts pre-Christian people in significant numbers, and experiences conversion growth? Let's consider perspectives from several other writers—Lyle Schaller, Ralph Neighbour, Rick Warren, and Melvin Steinbron.

1. Reaches new people

Culturally traditional churches do not develop and empower their people to reach postmodern people. Culturally relevant churches do.

Some of you have read "The Case for the Culturally Relevant Congregation" in my book *Church for the Unchurched*. Much of what I mean by cultural relevance can be effectively suggested through the acronym SLAM—the style, language, aesthetics, and music of the target population.

S   *S* has to do with style, which means variables like clothing style, leadership style, and interpersonal style.

L   *L* stands for language. We engage people through their language—their words, their dialect, their heart language—and by using words within their recognition vocabulary.

A   *A* stands for aesthetics, which involves adapting to their tastes in the fine arts, the folk arts, and architecture.

M   *M* stands for music. That's involved within their aesthetics, but it is so prominent today that it is probably the most indispensable single consideration.

Rick Warren has been saying for years, "Tell me what kind of music you feature in a particular worship service, and I will tell you who that worship service can reach and who that worship service will never reach."

Lyle Schaller's book *The Interventionist* demonstrates proof that a church's cultural orientation really does matter. He contends that virtually every denomination brought to the U.S.A. by people born and reared in Europe is now declining. Conversely, virtually every denomination that was made in America is growing. He supports his idea of the differences between European and American roots by listing a wide range of specific factors that contribute to a church's decline, stagnation, or growth. To illustrate Schaller's interesting idea, consider the 15 items in his much longer list:

European Cultural Roots	**Made in America**
Emphasizes First Person of Trinity	Second or Third Person
Intellectual approach	Experiential approach
The church is the real estate	The church is the people
Hierarchical organization	Flat organization
Large groups, attend programs	Small groups, know one another
Ministry of the clergy and staff	Ministry of the laity
Formality, titles	Informality, no titles
Past orientation	Future orientation
Music written before 1960 (or 1860, or 1760)	Music written after 1960 (or 1970, or 1980)

Focus on traditional liturgy	Focus on people's needs
Value stable institutions and continuity	Ad hoc organization, achievement
Keep dying churches/ institutions alive	Euthanasia! Move to opportunity
The worship service: if two— identical	Multiple worship services, different
The existing churches	New church planting
If start new ministries— subsidize	Autonomous and self-supporting

All this is a way of saying that employing a style, language, aesthetic, and music that is appropriate in American culture is the first step to winning unchurched people. Since the U.S.A. also has regional cultures, generational cultures, and many subcultures, Christianity's forms must be and can be shaped in many different culturally relevant ways. This is imperative because most secular people will not assume that Christianity is intended for people like them unless it is packaged in a way that is consistent with their cultural orientation.

This delivery system for the gospel is as old as the New Testament period. Jesus left the culture of the Trinity and adapted to a first-century, Galilean, Aramaic-speaking culture. Christianity has expanded through cultural adaptation ever since.

2. Programs vs. small groups

Churches that major in programs for people to attend do not develop and empower their people and reach secular, postmodern people. Churches that involve their people and seekers in small groups do. Ralph Neighbor, in books like *Where Do We Go from Here?* champions the small-group movement. Neighbor was one of the first to talk, not about churches *with* small groups, but about churches *of* small groups.

Ralph Neighbor contends that the program-based designed (PBD) church is a spent force. He believes this form of church, which we inherited from the Reformation, once fit the European culture when everyone lived in or near villages. That form of church, where people already had a close supportive network, understandably featured a church building, a pastor, and a flock gathered for worship from the parish area.

Neighbor contends that that inherited form has become increasingly ineffective in urban societies everywhere, especially in North America. The PBD church is now impotent because people do not live in villages or near their extended families. *Churchianity* is slowly dying from the program-based design because it hinders intimacy, support, and fellowship.

S mall groups must now provide the oikos, that is, the experience of belonging and being known.

Strategic churches, Neighbor says, now need to feature small-group life as the indispensable component of the local Christian movement. Small groups must now provide the *oikos,* that is, the experience of belonging and being known. They must take the place of supportive, nurturing, ministering-to-each-other networks that medieval society once automatically provided for people. The need is pressing because modern urban society no longer provides such important human connections.

Neighbor contends the PBD church assembles people in large groups, which prohibits people from experiencing any deep sense of community or belonging. Moreover, the PBD design confines most activities to the church building rather than encouraging the church's penetration into the community.

The PBD design consumes enormous time and energy for laypersons as well as clergy. That makes it improbable that the people will befriend or win many pre-Christian people. Indeed, Neighbor observes that the typical PBD church has limited contact with the unreached community.

Neighbor also makes a strong case that the PBD church does not build people but builds programs. Though leaders assume that programs build people, they usually do not achieve this goal. In fact, PBD churches usually produce wimpy, nominal, inactive members. So inactives typically number 40 to 50 percent of the PBD church's membership. Of those, half may attend monthly; the other half don't come at all.

Worst of all, life in the PBD church does not provide *koinonia* or fellowship, which is needed to create a true Christian community where people experience intimacy and build up one another. This is Neighbor's clincher:

> There is literally no time or place in a program-based church for people to become close to one another. Indeed, the programs isolate members from each other. When they meet, it's in the neutral setting of the church building. Each encounter is carefully programmed. There's choir music to be rehearsed, a Bible lesson to be studied, a budget to be prepared. Bonding together in love and commitment isn't possible. There's no community in the PBD church structure. Those who create community must do so in spite of the organization's schedule and are subject to criticism for not being cooperative with the church program (51).

Why Small Groups?

The following principles and strategies stem from Ralph Neighbor's books and from many other sources on small groups.

1. The viable church of the future will be a church of small groups, not merely a church with small groups.

2. Most small groups will meet in the community, thereby providing one way for the church to penetrate the community with the gospel.

3. Each small group will feature an empty chair or two for pre-Christian people. One of the group's goals is to fill that empty chair with a seeker or new believer every six months.

4. Each small group will be lay led. Often the small-group leader serves as the pastoral caregiver for the group members.

5. Each small group is training an assistant group leader who will one day lead a group.

6. When the small group grows beyond 12 or 15, it spawns a new group. The multiplication of groups has proven much more effective than dividing groups. So 2 or 3 members of a group go out and inseminate a new group for new people who are not involved in any group.

7. The church provides continuing training and support for group leaders. They are given a lot of recognition for doing the most important work of the church.

3. Governance vs. ministry by laity

Churches that involve their people in committee work and

governance do not develop and empower them to reach secular, postmodern people. Churches that deploy their people in ministries for which they are suited successfully accomplish their mission.

The necessity of employing laity in ministry is championed by Rick Warren in *The Purpose-Driven Church*. He straightforwardly states his belief based on experience: "Your church will never be any stronger than its core of lay ministers who carry out the various ministries of the church. Every church needs an intentional, well-planned system for uncovering, mobilizing, and supporting the giftedness of its members" (367).

Warren's rationale is that laypeople have limited time available, so the church has to choose whether to deploy laity in ministry or in maintenance. Do they do good church work or the work of the church?

Warren's suggestion to the churches of America is to deploy laity in ministries and to deploy staff in administration. Laypeople involved in committee work and governance are virtually never fulfilled, but laypeople involved in ministries for which they are gifted are deeply fulfilled. Don't let laity get bogged down in committees, meetings, governance, and church work. Warren contends staff should not be doing ministry for the laity. Rather, the staff should be leading and feeding the laity to do their ministry.

To develop this idea, Saddleback Church features a four-hour 301 seminar that helps people discover which of Saddleback's 110 ministries they should be involved in. The four-hour seminar is built around the acronym SHAPE.

S S stands for spiritual gifts. Within an hour or so, they discover with high probability what their spiritual gift mix is.

H H stands for heart. Out of all the things Saddleback Church does, individuals are helped to clarify which ones they think are most important or have a heart for.

A A stands for abilities. This session helps people identify their abilities—what they do well, with high motivation.

P P stands for personality. Saddleback Church uses an adapted form of the Myers-Briggs personality-type inventory to help people discover their personality traits. They are also taught how those traits impact their service for Christ.

E E stands for experiences. A lengthy session helps people reflect upon their experiences. Specifically, they focus on life experiences, educational experiences, vocational experiences, and painful experiences. They discover how the living God has been working through their experiences to prepare them to be more useful in the Kingdom.

Saddleback has discovered that God especially prepares people through painful experiences to minister to others who are experiencing a similar struggle. In Saddleback's recovery ministry, for example, virtually everybody who leads a 12-step group is himself or herself a person in recovery.

The ministry of many laity can also include basic pastoral care. Melvin Steinbron, in *Can the Pastor Do It Alone?* reports that the good news is that laypeople in significant numbers are shaped by God for a shepherding ministry. With some training, these laypeople can do 90 percent of what a theologically trained and ordained clergyperson can do, and sometimes better! The lay pastors movement has demonstrated that in any church, enough laypeople can be identified, trained, and deployed to do virtually all of the ongoing pastoral care of the members, especially in four expressions, suggested by the acronym PACE.

P P means the lay shepherd prays for every person in his or her group of 12 to 16 people.

A Available is the second commitment. Some lay shepherds are even available by cellular phone, beeper, or E-mail.

C C suggests that the lay shepherd contacts each group member at least weekly, by telephone or a drop-by.

E E stands for Christian example. The group leader provides a model of what it means to live the Christian life by the power of God.

AUTHENTIC MINISTRY DEVELOPS LAY CHRISTIANS

Churches of small groups that provide culturally relevant worship, deploy the members in SHAPE-based ministries, and train the people for outreach to pre-Christian people thereby produce an apostolic people and a church that experiences significant conversion growth. *Why* does this "apostolic" way of doing church produce an outreaching people?

When the church provides a worship service that outsiders can relate to, the members are more likely to invite seekers to share in the experience.

When laypeople are involved in a small group where they regularly talk about the gospel and what God is doing in their lives, they are much more likely to talk about these matters with pre-Christian people.

When people are involved in a ministry for which they are shaped, they are more likely to also exercise the ministry of evangelism.

When people are receiving regular pastoral care, they are more likely to engage in outreach.

When people are regular pastoral caregivers, they are enormously more likely to offer pastoral care and the ministry of Christian witness in their contacts with pre-Christian people.

For such reasons, the culturally relevant church that involves its people in small groups and SHAPE-based ministry produces a people who are more contagious, who engage in more outreach than most traditional churches dream of producing.

The wonderful but audacious mission statement of Willow Creek Community Church provides an appropriate summary for this chapter: "Our mission is to help irreligious people become fully devoted followers of Jesus Christ."

Afterword

The one quality we see in all cutting-edge churches the world over is a passion to reach the unchurched secular person. I started in my first pastorate, planting a church in Columbus, Ohio, by asking the soul-wrenching question: "How do we reach unchurched people?" This concern arose out of my knee-knocking experience of going door to door and meeting all kinds of people.

This poem, written by the Episcopal priest who helped Alcoholics Anonymous founder Bill Wilson, has been and continues to be my lifetime testimony of how I want to live. I hope it will be an inspiration to you for what you can do to reach unchurched people.

I STAND BY THE DOOR
An Apologia for My Life
Samuel Moor Shoemaker

I stand by the door.
I neither go too far in, nor stay too far out.
The door is the most important door in the world—
It is the door through which men walk when they find God.
There's no use in my going way inside, and staying there,
When so many are still outside and they, as much as I,
Crave to know where the door is.
And all that so many ever find
Is only the wall where a door ought to be.
They creep along the wall like blind men,
With outstretched, groping hands.
Feeling for a door, knowing there must be a door,
Yet they never find it . . .
So I stand by the door.

The most tremendous thing in the world
Is for men to find that door—the door to God.

The most important thing any man can do
Is to take hold of one of those blind, groping hands,
And put it on the latch—the latch that only clicks
And opens to the man's own touch.
Men die outside that door, as starving beggars die
On cold nights in cruel cities in the dead of winter—
Die for want of what is within their grasp.
They live, on the other side of it—live because they have not
found it.
Nothing else matters compared to helping them find it.
And open it, and walk in, and find Him . . .
So I stand by the door.

Go in, great saints, go all the way in—
Go way down into the cavernous cellars,
And way up into the spacious attics—
It is a vast, roomy house, this house where God is.
Go into the deepest of hidden casements,
Of withdrawal, of silence, of sainthood.
Some must inhabit those inner rooms,
And know the depths and heights of God,
And call outside to the rest of us how wonderful it is.
Sometimes I take a deeper look in,
Sometimes venture in a little farther;
But my place seems closer to the opening . . .
So I stand by the door.

There is another reason why I stand there.
Some people get part way in and become afraid
Lest God and the zeal of His house devour them;
For God is so very great, and asks all of us.
And these people feel a cosmic claustrophobia,
And want to get out. "Let me out!" they cry.
And the people way inside only terrify them more.
Somebody must be watching for the frightened
Who seek to sneak out just where they came in.

The people too far in do not see how near these are
To leaving—preoccupied with the wonder of it all.

Somebody must watch for those who have entered the door,
But who would like to run away. So for them, too,
I stand by the door.

I admire the people who go way in.
But I wish they would not forget how it was
Before they got in. Then they would be able to help
The people who have not yet even found the door,
Or the people who want to run away again from God.
You can go in too deeply, and stay in too long,
And forget the people outside the door.
As for me, I shall take my old accustomed place,
Near enough to God to hear Him, and know He is there,
But not so far from men as not to hear them,
And remember they are there, too.
Where? Outside the door—
Thousands of them, millions of them.
But—more important for me—
One of them, two of them, ten of them,
Whose hands I am intended to put on the latch.
So I shall stand by the door and wait
For those who seek it.
"I had rather be a doorkeeper . . ."
So I stand by the door.*

*Helen Smith Shoemaker, *I Stand By the Door: The Life of Sam Shoemaker* (New York: Harper and Row, 1967), ix-x.